HOTEL AND HOSPITALITY MANAGEMENT HOUSEKEEPING

HOTEL AND HOSPITALITY MANAGEMENT
HOUSEKEEPING

Editor
Prakash Talwar

ISHA

ISHA BOOKS

DELHI-110033

Hotel and Hospitality Management : Housekeeping

ISBN: 9788182053380

Published in 2006 in India by
Isha Books
D-43, Prithviraj Road,
Adarsh Nagar, Delhi-110033
e-mail : ishabooks@hotmail.com

Laser Typesetting at : Shiva Infosystem, Delhi
Printed at : Mehra Offset Press, Delhi

Preface

Housekeeping is the maintenance of a clean environment, usually in a house, but it also applies to industrial, commercial, and institutional settings. Management of a housekeeping operation entails scheduling staff, deliveries, services and maintenance, budget analysis, cost-controls and compliance with regulations. A well-run housekeeping department is integral to the success of any lodging operation.

As downsizing practices in the hospitality industry usher in leaner management and fewer operational levels, the role of executive housekeeper is undergoing a dramatic change. Today, the ideal executive housekeeper must be prepared to be a first-line manager—capable of running a housekeeping department with little or no intervention from upper management.

This book offers future industry professionals the tools they need to be competitive in this new era—the skills to manage resources, administer assets, and manage all of the technical operations of a busy housekeeping department. It demonstrates clearly how theoretical concepts apply to real-life situations.

Editor

Contents

1

Lodging Services

People who travel and stay away from home for more than a day need lodging mainly for sleeping. Other purposes are safety, shelter from cold and rain, having a place to store lugguage and being able to take a shower. They do that in a hotel, hostel or hostal, a private home (commercially, i.e. a bed and breakfast or guest house place, or non-commercially, with members of hospitality services or in the home of friends), in a tent, caravan/ camper (often on a campsite). In addition there are make-shift solutions.

A hotel is an establishment that provides lodging, usually on a short-term basis. Hotels often provide a number of additional guest services such as a restaurant, a swimming pool or childcare. Some hotels have conference services and encourage groups to hold conventions and meetings at their location. Hotels differ from motels in that most motels have drive-up, exterior entrances to the rooms, while hotels tend to have interior entrances to the rooms

The word hotel derives from the French hôtel, which originally referred to a French version of a townhouse, not a place offering accommodation (in contemporary usage, hôtel has the meaning of "hotel", and hôtel particulier is used for the old meaning). The French spelling (with the circumflex) was once also used in English, but is now rare. The circumflex replaces the 's' once preceding the 't' in the earlier hostel spelling, which over time received a new, but closely related meaning.

Basic accommodation of a room with a bed, a cupboard, a small table and a washstand only has largely been replaced by rooms with en-suite bathrooms and climate control. Other features found may be a telephone, an alarm clock, a TV, and broadband Internet connectivity. Food and drink may be supplied by a mini-bar (which often includes a small refrigerator) containing snacks and drinks (to be paid for on departure), and tea and coffee making facilities (cups, spoons, an electric kettle and sachets containing instant coffee, tea bags, sugar, and creamer or milk).

The cost and quality of hotels are usually indicative of the range and type of services available. Due to the enormous increase in tourism worldwide during the last decades of the 20th century, standards, especially those of smaller establishments, have improved considerably. For the sake of greater comparability, rating systems have been introduced, with the one to five stars classification being most common.

One of the most critical challenges facing lodging managers today is the development of a responsive organizational structure that is committed to quality. The organizing process of a lodgind establishment involves dividing tasks into jobs, specifying the appropriate department for each job, determining the optimum number of jobs in each department, and delegating authority within and among departments. The framework of jobs and departments that make up any organization must be directed toward achieving the organization's objectives.

JOB SPECIALIZATION

As there are types of lodging organizations, there are as many degrees of job specialization within the lodging industry. One extreme is the case of a hotel where the owner/operator is responsible for checking in the guests, servicing their needs, taking care of the housekeeping for the guest rooms, maintaining the building and grounds, and checking out the guests. There is, to be sure, much to recommend this method of work. It is rewarding to have total control over a project from beginning to end, and many people find it motivating to see the results of their efforts. However, as the demand for additional products or services increases, it becomes more and more difficult for an individual to do his or her job well. One benefit of the increased workload is increased revenue, which would enable the individual hotel operator to add housekeeping staff, one or more front desk agents to check in and check out the additional guests, and engineering and maintenance personnel to care for the building and grounds.

Specialization increases worker productivity and efficiency. On the other hand, delegating jobs increases the need for managerial control and coordination. Someone has to make sure that housekeeping staff come in after the painters have repainted a roo, not before! A crucial element of hotel and lodging management is coordinating the many specialized functions within hotels so that the organization runs smoothly.

Specialization has its own set of problems; it can result in workers performing the same tasks over and over again. A point can be reached where the degree of specialization so narrows a job's scope that the worker finds little joy or satisfaction in it. Signs of overspecialization include workers' loss of interest, lowered morale, increasing error rate, and reduction in service and product quality. One solution to this problem is to modify jobs so that teams can perform them. Instead of a single guest room attendant being assigned to a group of rooms, a work team in a hotel housekeeping department might clean all of the rooms on a particular floor.

Some establishments use teams regularly throughout the organization; others use teams more selectively. Teams can be directed by a manager or can be selfmanaged. The idea behind self-managed work teams is for workers to become their own managers, which increases their self-reliance as well as develops a talent pool. A concept called the quality circle is based on the belief that the people who actually do the work, rather than their managers, are the ones who are best able to identify, analyze, and correct problems they encounter. The quality circle is a group of employees, usually fewer than ten, who perform similar jobs and meet once per week to discuss their work, identify problems, and present possible solutions to those problems.

Role of General Manager (GM)

The general manager (GM) is responsible for defining and interpreting the policies established by top management. The general manager serves as a liaison to the hotel's owner or corporate parent, sets (or communicates) the overall strategic course of the hotel, sets hotel-wide goals, coordinates activities between departments, and arbitrates interdepartmental disputes. It is common practice in a large, full-service hotel for a director of public relations to report directly to the GM. The GM also has corporate-level responsibilities, participates on civic boards and committees, and engages in industry-related activities such as serving on the local tourism commission or hotel-motel association. In addition to possessing a high level of technical skill, the general manager must also be decisive, analytical, and skilled with both computers and people. He or she must be able to see the big picture and how all of the parts of the hotel fit into the overall organisation.

Role of Resident Manager

An executive may be promoted to relieve the general manager of some operational duties. This is often accomplished by elevating the duties and responsibilities of one particular department head without relieving that person of regular departmental duties. The title of this position is usually resident manager. It is quite common (and logical) for the general manager to select the manager of the rooms department to be resident manager.

Responsibilities of the resident manager include serving as acting GM in the GM's absence, representing the GM on interdepartmental hotel committees, and taking responsibility for important special projects such as major hotel renovations, VIP guests, and operating reports that require in-depth analysis for the regional or corporate offices.

Responsibilities of Rooms Department

Responsibilities of the rooms department include reservations, guest reception, room assignment, tracking the status of rooms, prompt forwarding of mail and phone messages, security, housekeeping of guest rooms and public spaces such as lobbies, and answering guests' questions. To perform these many duties effectively, the rooms department may be divided into a number of specialized subunits. To complicate matters, in many instances these subunits are also referred to as departments.

The laundry department is responsible for cleaning and pressing all the hotel's linens and employee uniforms as well as guest laundry. Because of its specialized function, little of the knowledge and skills required to manage a laundry operation is transferable to other areas of hotel operations. The front office is one of the most important departments in a hotel, as it often offers the only contact between guests and staff. A hotel's front office is where guests are greeted when they arrive, where they are registered and assigned to a room, and where they check out.

Usually, the telephone operator, other guest communications functions, and the bell staff or those employees responsible for delivering luggage and messages and attending to special guest requests also fall under the front office umbrella. The reservations department takes and tracks the hotel's future bookings. The housekeeping department is responsible for cleaning guest rooms and public spaces. Because of their specialized nature, the security and engineering departments are discussed in separate sections. A great deal of interdependence exists among the subunits of the rooms department. The front office must let reservations know whenever walk-in guests register. A similar level of cooperation is required between the front office and housekeeping. When a guest checks out, the front office must inform housekeeping so that the room may be cleaned. Once a room is cleaned, housekeeping must inform the front office so that the room may be sold. Certain tasks within the rooms department must occur in a specific order.

Housekeeping cannot properly provision a guest room if the laundry does not supply enough clean towels or bed sheets. Engineering cannot replace a defective light switch in a guest room if housekeeping does not report the problem. Effective management of this busy department calls for standardized plans, procedures, schedules, and deadlines, as well as frequent direct communication between the executives who manage the key operating units of the rooms department.

The hotel and lodging business is vulnerable to security and safety problems. Problems can be created by guests, employees, or intruders. Security breaches can result in embezzlement, theft, arson, robbery, and even terrorism. Depending on the size of a hotel or a lodging establishment, the security function may be handled by a fully staffed department on site, contracted to an outside security company, or assigned to designated staff members sonnel in the rooms department.

In a larger, full-service hotel, the director of security may report directly to the general manager. In smaller hotels, the security function might become a task of the rooms department. Engineering department's responsibilities include preventive maintenance; repair; replacement; improvement and modification to furniture, fixtures, and equipment (FFE); and ensuring uninterrupted provision of utilities (gas, electricity, water).Preventive maintenance involves routine checks and inspection of the key components of all equipment.

Maintenance of recreational facilities may be part of the engineering department's responsibilities. In particular, swimming pools require extensive maintenance to ensure proper filtration and to prevent the accumulation of algae and other conditions unsuitable for swimming. Prompt repair minimizes loss of productivity in other hotel operating departments and inconvenience to hotel guests. When a particular FFE has reached the end of its useful life and repair is no longer cost-effective, replacement is indicated. Improvement projects enhance the existing operation or reduce operating costs of the facility.

Modification projects alter the existing operation to accommodate one or more new functions. One hotel might have a large engineering staff that includes plumbers, carpenters, painters, electricians, and other technicians. Another might have maintenance personnel who have general knowledge and understanding of the hotel's operations but rely on outside contractors for specialized jobs. In larger, full-service hotels, engineering may be a separate department, with a director who reports directly to the resident manager.

Responsibilities of Food and Beverage Department

The primary function of the food and beverage department is to provide food and drink to a hotel's guests. In earlier times, when an inn had a single dining room that could hold a limited number of guests, this was a fairly simple task. Today, however, providing food and drink is much more complicated. A large hotel might well have a coffee shop, a gourmet restaurant, a poolside snack bar, room service, two banquet halls, and ten function rooms where food and beverages are served. It might also have a lounge, a nightclub, and a lobby bar. On a busy day, it's quite likely that functions will be booked in many outlets at the same time.

In addition, some outlets may have multiple events scheduled for a single day. As you can see, there is great diversity in the types of activities performed by a food and beverage department, requiring a significant variety of skills on the part of its workers. Because of the diversity of services provided, the food and beverage department is typically split into subunits. The executive chef, a person of considerable importance and authority in any full-service hotel, runs the food production, or kitchen, department.

A variety of culinary specialists who are responsible for different aspects of food preparation report to the executive chef. The actual serving of food in a large hotel's restaurants is usually the responsibility of a separate department, headed by the assistant food and beverage director. The food service department is composed of the individual restaurant and outlet managers, maitre d's, waiters, waitresses, and bus help. Because of their special duties and concerns, many large hotels have a separate subunit that is responsible only for room service. Because of the high value and profit margins associated with the sale of alcoholic beverages, some hotels have a separate department that assumes responsibility for all outlets where alcoholic beverages are sold.

The person responsible for this department is the beverage manager. Most full-service hotels also do a considerable convention and catering business. The typical convention uses small function rooms for meetings and larger rooms for general sessions, trade shows, exhibits, and banquets. As a hotel or lodging business increases the use of its facilities for conventions and meetings, it may form a separate convention services department.

The convention services department and its personnel are introduced to the client, a meeting planner, or an association executive by the marketing and sales department. The convention services department then handles all of the client's meeting and catering requirements. Individually catered events include parties, wedding receptions, business meetings, and other functions held by groups. To provide for the unique needs of these types of customers, hotels often organise separate catering and convention departments. Depending on the size of the hotel, the job of cleaning the food and beverage outlets themselves as well as of washing pots and pans, dishes, glasses, and utensils is often delegated to a subunit known as the stewarding department. It is only through continuous cooperation and coordination that a hotel's food service function can be carried out effectively.

A guest who is dining in a hotel restaurant requires the joint efforts of the kitchen, food service, beverage, and stewarding departments. A convention banquet cannot be held without the efforts of the convention and catering department along with the food production, beverage, and stewarding departments. The sequence of events and cooperation required among the food and beverage staff is even more important than in the rooms department, thus increasing the importance of communication between managers and employees alike. Another challenge faced by management is the diversity of the employees in the food and beverage department; the dishwasher in the stewarding department is at a dramatically different level than the sous chef in the kitchen. The primary responsibility of the sales managers who make up the marketing and sales department is sales, or the selling of the hotel facilities and services to individuals and groups. Sales managers sell rooms, food, and beverages to potential clients through advertising, attendance at association and conference meetings, and direct contacts.

Functions of Marketing and Sales Department

The marketing and sales department is removed from most of the day-to-day operational problems faced by other departments. The division of work among the sales managers is based on the type of customers a hotel is attempting to attract. Individual sales managers often specialize in corporate accounts, conventions, or tour and travel markets. Sales managers' accounts are sometimes subdivided along geographical lines into regional or national accounts.

Functions of Human Resource Department

The three functions of the human resources department are employee recruitment, benefits administration, and training. The director of human resources is also expected to be an expert on federal and state labor laws and to advise managers in other departments on these topics. The human resources department's major challenge is in its interactions with other hotel departments. Although the human resources department recruits, interviews, and screens prospective employees, the final hiring decision rests within the department in which the potential employee will be working. The same is true of promotion and disciplinary decisions; the human resources department's input is, in most cases, limited to advice and interpretation of legal questions. The human resources department's effectiveness depends on its manager's ability to form effective working relationships with managers of other departments.

Role of Accounting Department

The accounting department's traditional role is recording financial transactions, preparing and interpreting financial statements, and providing the managers of other departments with timely reports of operating results. The accounting department combines staff functions and line functions, or those functions directly responsible for servicing guests. Other responsibilities, carried out by the assistant controller for finance, include payroll preparation, accounts receivable, and accounts payable. Another dimension of the accounting department's responsibilities deals with various aspects of hotel operations, cost accounting, and cost control throughout the hotel. The two areas of central concern to the accounting department are rooms and food and beverage.

The accounting department's front office cashier is responsible for tracking all charges to guest accounts. At the close of each business day, which varies by hotel but typically occurs at midnight or after the bulk of guests' transactions have been completed, the night auditor is responsible for reconciling all guest bills with the charges from the various hotel departments. Although the front office cashier and the night auditor physically work at the front desk and, in the case of the cashier, have direct contact with guests, they are members of the accounting department and report to the assistant controller of operations.

The food and beverage department may be responsible for food preparation and service, but the accounting department is responsible for collecting revenues. The food and beverage controller and the food and beverage cashiers keep track of both the revenues and expenses of the food and beverage department. The food and beverage controller's job is to verify the accuracy and reasonableness of all food and beverage revenues. In addition to tracking and preparing daily reports on the costs of the food and beverages used in the hotel, in many cases the accounting department is also responsible for purchasing and storeroom operations. Finally, the director of systems is responsible for designing the accounting and control systems used throughout the hotel.

The accounting department is anything but a passive staff unit contending with routine recordkeeping. The accounting department is also responsible for collecting and reporting most of a hotel's operational and financial statistics, which provide important data for decision making and budget preparation purposes. The head of the accounting department may report not only to the hotel's general manager but also to the hotel chain's financial vice president or to the hotel's owner. The reason for this dual responsibility and reporting relationship is to afford the hotel corporation an independent verification of the financial and operating results of the hotel.

Authority

Authority is the organisationally sanctioned right to make a decision. Authority can be distributed throughout an organisation or held in the hands of a few select employees. The delegation of authority creates a chain of command, the formal channel that defines the lines of authority from the top to the bottom of an organisation.

The chain of command specifies a clear reporting relationship for each person in the organisation and should be followed in both downward and upward communication. Following the chain of command enables each new employee, no matter what his or her position, to know exactly for whom and to whom he or she is responsible.

When designing an organisational structure, managers must consider the distribution of authority. Decentralization is the process of distributing authority throughout an organisation. In a decentralized organisation, an organisation member has the right to make a decision without obtaining approval from a higher-level manager. Centralization is the retention of decision-making authority by a high-level manager. Traditionally, hotel and lodging management has been very centralized, probably due to its roots in small, owner-operated lodging.

In recent years, as the hotel and lodging industry has expanded, decentralization has become a more frequent style of operation. Decentralization has several advantages. Managers are encouraged to develop decision-making skills, which help them advance in their careers. The autonomy afforded by this style of operation also increases job satisfaction and motivation. When employees are encouraged to perform well, the profitability of the organisation increases.

Many hotel and lodging organisations have begun to empower employees and supervisors to make decisions that typically have been made by managers. One example that we have already discussed is the use of the quality circle. For example, if a front desk agent determines that a guest's bill is incorrect, in a decentralized organisation the agent has the power to make the correction immediately. If that same front desk agent determines that a guest's stay has been unsatisfactory, he or she has the power to reduce the guest's bill by an amount previously specified by management. Additional challenges, control of the process, and quality assessment become part of everyone's job, and each employee is given the authority to take positive actions that will lead to high quality and improved performance.

Controlling the Organisation

It refers to the number of people who report to one manager or supervisor. A wide span of control results in a flat organisation that is, a large number of employees reporting to one supervisor. A narrow span of control results in a tall organisation, in which a small number of employees report to a supervisor, necessitating a larger number of supervisors. No formula exists for determining the ideal span of control.

The factors determine the most appropriate span of control are: task similarity, training and professionalism, task certainty, frequency of interaction, task integration, and physical dispersion. When a large number of employees perform similar tasks, the span of control can be increased. When the employees perform very different tasks, the supervisor must give each subordinate more individual attention in order to keep in touch with the different types of tasks; this requires a narrower span of control. For example, the rooms department manager might easily manage the front desk agents and housekeepers until the brand standards for check-in or checkout of a guest increase in complexity and the standards for the various types of rooms and their cleaning procedure increase in detail. At this time, the rooms department manager's span of control must be narrowed.

The better trained and more skilled a subordinate is, the less supervision is required. For example, a front desk agent might require a higher level of training and skill than a room service waiter. Thus, a front desk supervisor can supervise more employees (wider span of control) than the room service supervisor (narrower span of control). Task certainty refers to the predictability of a task. Routine tasks allow management to devise standard procedures for subordinates to follow, minimizing questions about the job and widening the span of control. On the other hand, close supervision is called for when tasks are ambiguous and uncertainty is great. For example, the task of checking a guest in or out of the hotel can be documented and standard procedures can be created, so the front desk manager can have a rel-atively wide span of control over the front desk agents. However, because of the diversity of customers the sales manager encounters, the tasks of a hotel sales manager are less certain. The director of sales is responsible for coaching the sales managers, observing sales calls, and ensuring deal closings; these tasks require a hands-on approach that limits the number of employees the director of sales can handle, narrowing the span of control.

If the supervisor-subordinate relationship requires frequent interaction, the span of control must be narrow. If interaction is infrequent, the span of control can be wide. For example, the hotel controller must review regularly the status of collections and payments with staff. In contrast, the frequency of interaction between the chief engineer and his or her subordinates is directed by written work orders in most circumstances and thus requires less direct communication, enabling a wider span of control.

If the supervisor must integrate and coordinate the tasks of subordinates, the span of control narrows. For example, in the production of a meal for one table of four guests with different appetizers, salads, and entrées, the chef must have a narrow span of control to ensure that each component of the meal is assembled correctly and delivered to service personnel on a timely basis. The span of control of the executive housekeeper can be much wider because the procedure for cleaning and preparing each guest room is similar, if not exactly the same, for every room.

Physical dispersion refers to the distribution of employees within the lodging establishment. For example, if the executive housekeeper has guest room attendants on 20 floors in two buildings and the front desk manager has all front desk agents located in one place, the span of control would narrow for the executive housekeeper and widen for the front desk manager. The ideal number of people that one person can supervise depends on a variety of factors. Consistent with trends in organisational structure such as teams, quality circles, and employee empowerment, many hotel and lodging organisations are widening their span of control. The objective behind these trends is to develop a flatter, more responsive organisational structure in which employees can make decisions without going through several levels of management.

One of the most important strength of a functional organisational design is efficiency. The performance of common tasks allows for work specialization, which increases overall productivity. Workers develop specialized skills and knowledge more rapidly. Training is easier because of the similarity of tasks and the resulting opportunities for inexperienced workers to learn from experienced workers. This helps new employees quickly learn the kinds of behavior that lead to success and promotion.

Coordination of activities within functional departments is easier than in more broadly based organisations. A functional organisation fosters efficiency, teamwork, and coordination of activities within individual units. However, the functional organisation's most important strength is also the source of its great-est shortcoming. The success of a hotel as a business is measured by its overall performance and not by the performance of any one department.

A hotel with spotless guest rooms will not be successful if guests' front desk experiences are not up to par. Even if guests' dining experiences are superb, the hotel will fall flat on its face if its rooms are dismal. It is sometimes difficult for each department to fully appreciate its role in the overall success of the organisation. It is vital that each department keep in mind the hotel-wide goals of customer service and profitability rather than focus narrowly on its own concerns. Some means must be found to coordinate the activities of functional departments and to set hotel-wide strategies and goals. A hotel's functional organisation demands strong leadership. New initiatives in hotels often require cooperation and coordination between functional departments. New ideas tend to be stillborn if department heads lack a hotel-wide perspective or have difficulty coordinating their activities.

The tendency to concentrate on doing things right often overshadows the organisation's ability to do the right thing.The GM, as the chief executive of the hotel, emerges as the single person capable of providing the overall organisational direction, decision making, coordination, and arbitration needed to make a hotel's functional departments work together effectively. A hotel simply cannot run itself from the departmental level. Thus, the GM must be a strong leader to be effective.

The executive operating committee (EOC) of a hotel, made up of the general manager and senior executives from each department, is designed to increase the level of coordination between departments. There is no standard membership for this committee, but it usually comprises those executives who report directly to the general manager. The EOC is also responsible for a hotel's major budgetary units, such as the food and beverage and housekeeping units. EOC functions depend on how the hotel GM chooses to use the group, the GM's style, and the structure of other management meetings in the hotel. Typically, the EOC meets weekly, focusing on matters ranging from day-today operational issues to comparing budgets with actual operating results.

Importance of Staff Meetings

Many hotels increase communications through an elaborate structure of additional committees and meetings, including some or all of the following: operations, staff, sales forecast and marketing, departmental, subdepartmental, credit, safety, energy conservation, and employee meetings. The operations committee comprises the general manager, department heads, front office manager, manager on duty, and representatives from housekeeping, security, engineering, and food and beverage. This committee might meet four or five times per week for 15 to 20 minutes to review upcoming activities and assess the results of previous activities. The staff committee might include the GM, department heads, and all subdepartment heads who report to the department heads. This committee, which might meet weekly for one or two hours, reviews the prior week's performance, the current week's activities, the next week's plans, and special projects. The staff committee also presents performance awards to employees.

The sales forecast and marketing committee might meet one to four times per month for several hours so the GM and department heads can review room demand for the coming 90 days and devise strategies to increase room nights (and thus bring in more revenue) and to increase average daily rates by up-selling potential guests to higher-rated rooms with perhaps more amenities or services. The departmental committee consists of the department head and his or her subdepartment heads, managers, and supervisors.

Meeting once or twice per month for an hour or so, the group reviews departmental issues. Similarly, subdepartment committees meet monthly for about an hour so the subdepartment head, managers, and supervisors can address issues unique to their subdepartment, such as the selection of a new type of floor cleaner by the housekeeping department or a more energy-efficient light bulb by the engineering department. The credit committee includes the general manager, the controller, sales, the front office, reservations, catering, and the credit manager. Meeting monthly for an hour, the committee reviews those guests and clients of the hotel who were granted credit but have not settled their account. The safety committee typically comprises representatives from human resources, food and beverage, housekeeping, and engineering. Meeting monthly for an hour or so, the committee reviews safety programs and safety records, addresses problems, and discusses the implementation of new safety regulations.

In some full-service hotels, an energy conservation committee includes the chief engineer, resident manager, food and beverage staff, human resource representatives, rooms staff, and housekeeping representatives. The committee typically meets monthly for an hour to discuss strategies and programs for controlling energy costs. Most full-service hotels convene a monthly meeting or at least an annual meeting of all hotel management and employees to review performance and to distribute awards. This event ranges from an hourlong meeting to a company-wide celebration lasting several hours.

As new business practices are evolving as fast as our technologies, resistance to change has become a primary cause of business failure. The future success of a hotel will be driven in large part by the ability to foresee and capitalize on change. As we go through global transitions, the successful hotel will examine the key factors that will not only define success but also the ability to survive in coming years. These key organisational trends must be acknowledged by the successful hotel organisation: visionary leadership, globalization, diversity, flexibility, flat structure, customer focus, zero defects, network orientation, and being in the information fast lane.

The organisation must be able to respond to increasingly globalized sales, the movement to maintaining sales offices in many countries and hotel properties across the globe, and an increasingly globalized labor market. Intercontinental Hotels Group recently introduced a new organisation structure to more efficiently use regional and global resources to drive higher levels of innovation, customer focus, and revenues. Diversity means the organisation must respond to a workforce that is heterogeneous sexually, racially, and chronologically; innovation and conflict/communication issues; and different styles of interaction, dress, presentation, and physical appearance. Flexibility in the modern hotel organisation means assuring that systems, processes, and people can respond differently to different situations; fewer detailed rules and procedures; greater autonomy and encouragement of initiative; customizing employment relationships to include telecommuting and job-sharing; and lifetime employability rather than lifetime employment. The trend toward flatness in hotel organisations means fewer levels of management, workers empowered to make decisions, and fewer differences in responsibility.

The organisation's employees need to believe in a sense of entrepreneurship that reacts proactively to market diversity. Traditional organisations that follow well-documented rules must give way to leaders who can balance a sense of discipline with one of flexibility. If the customer is king or queen in the 21st century, hotel organisaions will be best served by focusing less on their hotel assets as measures of success and more on their customers. This involves a fundamental shift from viewing the real estate asset as the wealth creator to seeing the customer as the key to building shareholder wealth.

A customer focus must reflect business decisions at all levels of developing and operating a hotel organisation. Pursuing such a course will inevitably impact shareholder wealth. Today's hotel organisation must recognize the need for visionary leadership. The old command-and-control model of leadership is giv-ing way to a focus on leadership in ideas, information, inspiration, vision, and teamwork.

A failing hotel organisation is overmanaged and underled. The networked hotel organisation can facilitate direct communication across unit and property boundaries, ignoring the chain of command; cross-unit team structures; outsourcing and downsizing; strategic alliances with competitors and others; customization; and decentralization.

Being in the information fast lane is critical. The traditional role of information technology as a back office support for accounting and bookkeeping has clearly moved to front and center stage. Information technology today influences all aspects of business from corporate strategies to organisational structure. Technology was once viewed as a way to reduce costs by replacing people. That attitude has been firmly supplanted by the idea of seeking information technology support for the creative work all organisations must pursue. Information technology must enable organisations to react more speedily to market needs and, of course, produce the fulfillment of customer demands both quickly and accurately. To do this it must operate on a decentralized basis. Information technology delivers, but it has to deliver the right information to the right people at the right time.

2

Staffing Operations

Staffing is one of a hotel's most important management functions, is an ongoing challenge because of the high rate of employee and manager turnover. Full-service hotels can experience annual turnover rates in excess of 100 percent in certain employee classifications. Some managers consider an annual employee turnover rate of 33 percent low. At this rate, the entire hotel must be completely restaffed every three years. The higher the turnover rate, the larger the number of employees who must be replaced. In an attempt to reduce employee turnover, hotel and lodging businesses are giving increasing attention to job design, seeking to enhance those job characteristics that give the employee the greatest satisfaction and motivation. Good job design must take into account the needs of employees as well as the demands of the job.

Well-thought-out job design begins when management conducts a job analysis-that is, a thorough evaluation of the specific tasks performed for a particular job and the time required to perform them. Job analysis is an ongoing process, as many jobs change with improvements in technology and pressure to improve product quality. The job analysis is the basis for the job description and job specification. A job description includes the job title, pay, a brief statement of duties and procedures, working conditions, and hours.

The job specification is an outline of the qualifications necessary for a particular job. In response to the limits of specialization, organisations can redesign jobs to improve coordination, productivity, and product quality while responding to an employee's needs for learning, challenge, variety, increased responsibility, and achievement. Such job redesign often involves job rotation, the systematic movement of employees from one job to another; job enlargement, an increase in the number of tasks an employee will do in the job; job enrichment, the attempt to give the employee more control over job-related activities; and flextime, a flexible work schedule that permits employee input in establishing work schedules. In team-driven job redesign, a concept similar to job rotation, employees can transfer back and forth among teams that provide different services or products.

Hotels recruit employees from a variety of sources. Newspapers and employee referrals are used to recruit nonskilled hourly employees. Supervisory and management employees generally are recruited through colleges and universities, promotions from within, professional associations, and management recruiters. Hotels that take more time in making their selections are more successful in retaining employees. Discussions of employee training and development often concentrate on training techniques without giving a full explanation of what a hotel is trying to accomplish. As training and development impart job skills and educate employees, supervisors, and managers, they also improve current and future employee performance, which affects the bottom line.

Effective training includes problem solving, problem analysis, quality measurement and feedback, and team building. Performance evaluation, also called performance appraisal, is the systematic review of the strengths and weaknesses of an employee's performance. The major difficulty in a performance appraisal is quantifying those strengths and weaknesses. The performance of some jobs is easy to quantify, while for others it is more difficult. An important part of the appraisal process is a well-established job description, so that the employee and the supervisor have similar expectations. Compensation includes the monetary and nonmonetary rewards that managers, supervisors, and employees receive for performing their jobs. In order to set compensation levels, the human resources department must periodically conduct job evaluations, which determine the value of the job to the hotel. Knowledge of the value of the job to the organisation and of wage rates for each job classification allows the hotel to establish a fair compensation policy.

There are several activities involved in staffing a housekeeping operation. Executive housekeepers must select and interview employees, participate in an orientation program, train newly hired employees, and develop employees for future growth.

Selection of Employees

Each region has its own demographic situations that affect the availability of suitable employees for involvement in housekeeping or environmental service operations. For example, in one area, an exceptionally high response rate from people seeking food service work may occur and a low response rate from people seeking housekeeping positions may occur. In another area, the reverse may be true, and people interested in housekeeping work may far outnumber those interested in food service.

Advertising campaigns that will reach these employees are the best method of locating suitable people. Major classified ads associated with mass hirings will specify the need for food service personnel, front desk clerks, food servers, housekeeping personnel, and maintenance people. Such ads may yield surprising results. If the volume of response for housekeeping personnel is insufficient to provide a suitable hiring base, the following sources may be investigated:

— Local employment agencies

— Flyers posted on community bulletin boards

— Local church organizations

— Neighborhood canvass for friends of recently hired employees

— Direct radio appeals to local homemakers

— Organizations for underprivileged ethnic minorities, and mentally disabled people

If these sources do not produce the volume of applicants necessary to develop a staff, it may become necessary to search for employees in distant areas and to provide regular transportation for them to and from work. If aliens are hired, the department manager must take great care to ensure that they are legal residents of this country and that their green cards are valid.

More than one hotel department manager has had an entire staff swept away by the Department of Immigration after hiring people who were illegal aliens. Such unfortunate action has required the immediate assistance of all available employees to fill in. Whether you are involved in a mass hiring or in the recruiting of a single employee, a systematic and courteous procedure for processing applicants is essential. For example, in the opening of the Los Angeles Airport Marriott, 11,000 applicants were processed to fill approximately 850 positions in a period of about two weeks. The magnitude of such an operation required a near assembly-line technique, but a personable and positive experience for the applicants still had to be maintained.

The efficient handling of lines of employees, courteous attendance, personal concern for employee desires, and reference to suitable departments for those unfamiliar with what the hotel or hospital has to offer all become earmarks for how the company will treat its employees. The key to proper handling of applicants is the use of a control system whereby employees are conducted through the steps of application, prescreening, and if qualified, reference to a department for interview. Even though an employee may desire involvement in one classification of work, he or she may be hired for employment in a different department. Also, employees might not be aware of the possibilities available in a particular department at the time of application or may be unable to locate in desired departments at the time of mass hirings.

Employees who perform well should therefore be given the opportunity to transfer to other departments when the opportunities arise. According to laws regulated by federal and state Fair Employment Practices Agencies (FEPA), no person may be denied the opportunity to submit application for employment for a position of his or her choosing. Not only is the law strict on this point, but companies in any way benefiting from interstate commerce may not discriminate in the hiring of people based on race, color, national origin, or religious preference. Although specific hours and days of the week may be specified, it is a generally accepted fact that hotels and hospitals must maintain personnel operations that provide the opportunity for people to submit applications without prejudice.

ORIENTATION

A carefully planned, concerned, and informational orientation program is significant to the first impressions that a new employee will have about the hospital or hotel in general and the housekeeping department in particular. Too often, a new employee is told where the work area and restroom are, given a cursory explanation of the job, then put to work. It is not uncommon to find managers putting employees to work who have not even been processed into the organization, an unfortunate situation that is usually discovered on payday when there is no paycheck for the new employee.

Such blatant disregard for the concerns of the employee can only lead to a poor perception of the company. A planned orientation program will eliminate this type of activity and will bring the employee into the company with personal concern and with a greater possibility for a successful relationship. A good orientation program is usually made up of four phases: employee acquisition, receipt of an employee's handbook, tour of the facility, and an orientation meeting.

Employee Acquisition

Once a person is accepted for employment, the applicant is told to report for work at a given time and place, and that place should be the personnel department. Preemployment procedures can take as much as one-half day, and department managers eager to start new employees to work should allow time for a proper employee acquisition into the organization.

At this time it should be ensured that the application is complete and any additional information pertaining to employment history that may be necessary to obtain the necessary work permits and credentials is on hand. Usually the security department records the entry of a new employee into the staff and provides instructions regarding use of employee entrances, removing parcels from the premises, and employee parking areas. Application for work permits, and drug testing, will be scheduled where applicable. All documents required by the hotel's health and welfare insurer should be completed, and instructions should be given about immediately reporting accidents, no matter how slight, to supervisors. The federal government requires that every employer submit a W-4 (withholding statement) for each employee on the payroll. Mandatory deductions from pay should be explained (federal and state income tax and Social Security FICA), as should other deductions that may be required or desired.

At this time, some form of personal action document is usually initiated for the new employee and is placed in the employee's permanent record. When a change has to be made, such as job title, marital status, or rate of pay, the PAF is retrieved from the employee's record, changes are made under the item to be changed, and the corrected PAF is used to change the data in the computer storage. Once new information is stored, a new PAF is created and placed in the employee's record to await the next need for processing. A long-time employee might have many PAFs stored in the personnel file.

Familiarization of Facilities

Upon completion of the acquisition phase, a facility tour should be conducted for one or all new employees. For new facilities, access to the property should be gained within about one week before opening, and many new employees can be taken on a tour simultaneously. It is possible for employees to work in the hotel housekeeping department for years and never to have visited the showroom, dining rooms, ballrooms, or even the executive office areas. A tour of the complete facility melds employees into the total organization, and a complete informative tour should never be neglected. For ongoing operations, after acquisition, the new employee may be turned over to a department supervisor, who becomes the tour director. An appreciation of the total involvement of each employee is strengthened when a facilities tour is complete and thorough. If necessary, the property tour might be postponed until after the orientation meeting; however, the orientation activity of staffing is not complete until a property tour is conducted.

Orientation Meeting

The orientation meeting should not be conducted until the employee has had an opportunity to become at least partially familiar with the surroundings. Employee orientation meetings that are scheduled too soon fail to answer many questions that will develop within the first two weeks of employment. The meeting should be held in a comfortable setting, with refreshments provided. It is usually conducted by the director of human resources and is attended by as many of the facility managers as possible.

Most certainly, the general manager or hospital administration members of the executive committee, the security director, and the new employees' department heads should attend. Each of these managers should have an opportunity to welcome the new employees and give them a chance to associate names with faces. All managers and new employees should wear name tags. In orientation meetings, a brief history of the company and company goals should be presented.

Although the new employee will be gaining confidence and security in the position as training ends and work is actually performed, informal orientation may continue for quite some time. The formal orientation, however, ends with the orientation meeting. Finally, it should be remembered that good orientation procedures lead to worker satisfaction and help quiet the anxieties and fears that a new employee may have. When a good orientation is neglected, the seeds of dissatisfaction are planted.

TRAINING

The efficiency and economy with which any department will operate will depend on the ability of each member of the organization to do his or her job. Such ability will depend in part on past experiences, but more commonly it can be credited to the type and quality of training offered. Employees, regardless of past experiences, always need some degree of training before starting a new job. Small institutions may try to avoid training by hiring people who are already trained in the general functions with which they will be involved. However,most institutions recognize the need for training that is specifically oriented toward the new experience, and will have a documented training program. Some employers of housekeeping personnel find it easier to train completely unskilled and untrained personnel. In such cases, bad or undesirable practices do not have to be trained out of an employee.

Previous experience and education should, however, be analyzed and considered in the training of each new employee in order that efficiencies in training can be recognized. If an understanding of department standards and policies can be demonstrated by a new employee, that portion of training may be shortened or modified. However, skill and ability must be demonstrated before training can be altered. Finally, training is the best method to communicate the company's way of doing things, without which the new employee may do work contrary to company policy.

First Training

First training of a new employee actually starts with a

continuation of department orientation. When a new employee is turned over to the housekeeping or environmental services department, orientation usually continues by familiarizing the employee with department rules and regulations. Many housekeeping departments have their own department employee handbooks.

Systematic Approach to Training

Training may be defined as those activities that are designed to help an employee begin performing tasks for which he or she is hired or to help the employee improve performance in a job already assigned. The purpose of training is to enable an employee to begin an assigned job or to improve upon techniques already in use. In hotel or hospital housekeeping operations, there are three basic areas in which training activity should take place: skills, attitudes, and knowledge.

Skills Training: A sample list of skills in which a basic housekeeping employee must be trained follows:

— *Bed making*: Specific techniques; company policy

— *Vacuuming*: Techniques; use and care of equipment

— *Dusting*: Techniques; use of products

— *Window and mirror cleaning*: Techniques and products

— *Setup awareness*: Room setups; what a properly serviced room should look like

— *Bathroom cleaning*: Tub and toilet sanitation; appearance; methods of cleaning and results desired

— *Daily routine*: An orderly procedure for the conduct of the day's work; daily communications

— *Caring for and using equipment*: Housekeeper cart; loading

— *Industrial safety*: Product use; guest safety; fire and other emergencies The best reference for the skills that require training is the job description for which the person is being trained.

Attitude Guidance: Employees need guidance in their attitudes about the work that must be done. They need to be guided in their thinking about rooms that may present a unique problem in cleaning. Attitudes among section housekeepers need to be such that, occasionally, when rooms require extra effort to be brought back to standard, it is viewed as being a part of rendering service to the guest who paid to enjoy the room.

The rooms are there to be enjoyed. Positive relationships with various agencies and people also need to be developed. The following is a list of areas in which attitude guidance is important:

— The guest/patient

— The department manager and immediate supervisor

— A guestroom that is in a state of great disarray

— The hotel and company

— The uniform

— Appearance

— Personal hygiene

Meeting Standards: The most important task of the trainer is to prepare new employees to meet standards. With this aim in mind, sequence of performance in cleaning a guestroom is most important in order that efficiency in accomplishing day-to-day tasks may be developed. In addition, the best method of accomplishing a task should be presented to the new trainee. Once the task has been learned, the next thing is to meet standards, which may not necessarily mean doing the job the way the person has been trained.

Ongoing Training

There is a need to conduct ongoing training for all employees, regardless of how long they have been members of the department. There are two instances when additional training is needed:

— the purchase of new equipment, and

— change in or unusual employee behavior while on the job.

When new equipment is purchased, employees need to know how the new equipment differs from present equipment, what new skills or knowledge are required to operate the equipment, who will need this knowledge, and when. New equipment may also require new attitudes about work habits.

Employee behavior while on the job that is seen as an indicator for additional training may be divided into two categories: events that the manager witnesses and events that the manager is told about by the employees. Events that the manager witnesses that indicate a need for training are frequent employee absence, considerable spoilage of products, carelessness, a high rate of accidents, and resisting direction by supervisors.

Events that the manager might be told about that indicate a need for training are that something doesn't work right, something is dangerous to work with, something is making work harder. Although training is vital for any organization to function at top efficiency, it is expensive. The money and man-hours expended must therefore be worth the investment. There must be a balance between the dollars spent training employees and the benefits of productivity and high-efficiency performance.

A simple method of determining the need for training is to measure performance of workers: Find out what is going on at present on the job, and match this performance with what should be happening. The difference, if any, describes how much training is needed. If the employee could not do the job even if his or her life depended on the outcome, there is a deficiency of knowledge (DK). If the employee could have done the job if his or her life depended on the outcome, but did not, there is a deficiency of execution (DE).

If either deficiency of knowledge or deficiency of execution exists, training must be conducted. The approach or the method of training may differ, however. Deficiencies of knowledge can be corrected by training the employee to do the job, then observing and correcting as necessary until the task is proficiently performed. Deficiency of execution is usually corrected by searching for the underlying cause of lack of performance, not by teaching the actual task.

Training Methods

There are numerous methods or ways to conduct training. Each method has its own advantages and disadvantages, which must be weighed in the light of benefits to be gained. Some methods are more expensive than others but are also more effective in terms of time required for comprehension and proficiency that must be developed. Several useful methods of training housekeeping personnel are listed and discussed.

On-the-Job Training: Using on-the-job training (OJT), a technique in which "learning by doing" is the advantage, the instructor demonstrates the procedure and then watches the students perform it. With this technique, one instructor can handle several students. In housekeeping operations, the instructor is usually a GRA who is doing the instructing in the rooms that have been assigned for cleaning that day. The OJT method is not operationally productive until the student is proficient enough in the training tasks to absorb part of the operational load.

Simulation Training: With simulation training, a model room (unrented) is set up and used to train several employees. Whereas OJT requires progress toward daily production of ready rooms, simulation requires that the model room not be rented. In addition, the trainer is not productive in cleaning ready rooms. The advantages of simulation training are that it allows the training process to be stopped, discussed, and repeated if necessary. Simulation is an excellent method, provided the trainer's time is paid for out of training funds, and clean room production is not necessary during the workday.

Coach-Pupil Method: The coach-pupil method is similar to OJT except that each instructor has only one student (a one-to-one relationship). This method is desired, provided that there are enough qualified instructors to have several training units in progress at the same time.

Lectures: The lecture method reaches the largest number of students per instructor. Practically all training programs use this type of instruction for certain segments. Unfortunately, the lecture method can be the dullest training technique, and therefore requires instructors who are gifted in presentation capabilities. In addition, space for lectures may be difficult to obtain and may require special facilities.

Conferences: The conference method of instruction is often referred to as workshop training. This technique involves a group of students who formulate ideas, do problem solving, and report on projects. The conference or workshop technique is excellent for supervisory training.

Demonstrations: When new products or equipment are being introduced, demonstrations are excellent. Many demonstrations may be conducted by vendors and purveyors as a part of the sale of equipment and products. Difficulties may arise when language barriers exist. It is also important that no more information be presented than can be absorbed in a reasonable period of time; otherwise misunderstandings may arise.

Training Aids

Many hotels use training aids in a conference room, or post messages on an employee bulletin board. Aside from the usual training aids such as chalkboards, bulletin boards, charts, graphs, and diagrams, photographs can supply clear and accurate references for how rooms should be set up, maids' carts loaded, and routines accomplished. Most housekeeping operations have films on guest contact and courtesy that may also be used in training. Motion pictures speak directly to many people who may not understand proper procedures from reading about them. Many training techniques may be combined to develop a well-rounded training plan.

Promotion to Improve Potential

It is possible to have two students sitting side by side in a classroom, with one being trained and the other being developed. Recall that the definition of training is preparing a person to do a job for which he or she is hired or to improve upon performance of a current job. Development is preparing a person for advancement or to assume greater responsibility.

The techniques are the same, but the end result is quite different. Whereas training begins after orientation of an employee who is hired to do a specific job, upon introduction of new equipment, or upon observation and communication with employees indicating a need for training, development begins with the identification of a specific employee who has shown potential for advancement. Training for promotion or to improve potential is in fact development and must always include a much neglected type of training -supervisory training. Many forms of developmental training may be given on the property; other forms might include sending candidates to schools and seminars. Developmental training is associated primarily with supervisors and managerial development and may encompass many types of experiences.

Development of individuals within the organization looks to future potential and promotion of employees. Specifically, those employees who demonstrate leadership potential should be developed through supervisory training for advancement to positions of greater responsibility. Unfortunately, many outstanding workers have their performance rewarded by promotion but are given no development training.

The excellent section housekeeper who is advanced to the position of senior housekeeper without the benefit of supervisory training is quickly seen to be unhappy and frustrated and may possibly become a loss to the department. It is therefore most essential that individual potential be developed in an orderly and systematic manner, or else this potential may never be recognized.

Even though there will be times that the trainee may be given specific responsibilities to oversee operations, clean guestrooms, or service public areas, advantage should not be taken of the trainee or the situation to the detriment of the development function. Development of new growth in the trainee becomes difficult when the training instructor or coordinator is not only developing a new manager but is also being held responsible for the production of some aspect of housekeeping operations.

Whether you are conducting a training or a development program, suitable records of training progress should be maintained both by the training supervisor and the student. Periodic evaluations of the student's progress should be conducted, and successful completion of the program should be recognized. Public recognition of achievement will inspire the newly trained or developed employee to achieve standards of performance and to strive for advancement.

Once an employee is trained or developed and his or her satisfactory performance has been recognized and recorded, the person should perform satisfactorily to standards. Future performance may be based on beginning performance after training. If an employee's performance begins to fall short of standards and expectations, there has to be a reason other than lack of skills.

The reason for unsatisfactory performance must then be sought out and addressed. This type of follow-up is not possible unless suitable records of training and development are maintained and used for comparison. Although evaluation and performance appraisal for employees will occur as work progresses, it is not uncommon to find the design of systems for appraisal as part of organization and staffing functions. This is true because first appraisal and evaluation occurs during training, which is an activity of staffing. Once trainees begin to have their performance appraised, the methods used will continue throughout employment. As a part of training, new employees should be told how, when, and by whom their performances will be evaluated, and should be advised that questions regarding their performance will be regularly answered.

Probationary Period

Initial employment should be probationary in nature, allowing the new employee to improve efficiency to where the designated number of rooms cleaned per day can be achieved in a probationary period (about three months). Should a large number of employees be unable to achieve the standard within that time, the standard should be investigated. Should only one or two employees be unable to meet the standard of rooms cleaned per day, an evaluation of the employee in training should either reveal the reason why or indicate the employee as unsuitable for further retention. An employee who, after suitable training, cannot meet a reasonable performance standard should not be allowed to continue employment. Similarly, an employee who has met required performance standards in the specified probationary period should be continued into regular employment status and thus achieve a reasonable degree of security in employment.

Evaluation of Personnel

Evaluation of personnel is an attempt to measure selected traits, characteristics, and productivity. Unfortunately, evaluations are generally objective in nature, and raters are seldom trained in the art of subject've evaluation. Initiative, self-control, and leadership ability do not lend themselves to measurement; therefore such characteristics are estimated. How well they are estimated depends to a great extent on the person doing the estimating.

Certain policies on the use of evaluations should be established so that they are understood by both the person doing the evaluating and the person being evaluated. These policies must be established and disseminated by management. Evaluation should be used at the end of a probationary period, and the employee must understand at the beginning of the period that he or she will be observed and evaluated. Each item, as well as what impact the evaluation will have on future employment, should be explained to the employee. People undergoing periodic evaluations, such as at the end of one year's employment, should also know why evaluations are being conducted and what may result from the evaluation. In both situations, the evaluation should be used for counseling and guidance so that performance may be improved upon or corrected if necessary. Certainly, strong points should be pointed out.

In certain locales, such as isolated resorts, hotels are tempted to use contract labor because the local market does not support the necessary number of workers, particularly in housekeeping. Advocates of outsourcing are quick to point out the advantages of the practice. Scarce workers are provided to the property, and there is no need to provide expensive employee benefits.

The entire staffing function is assumed by the contractor. There are no worries regarding recruiting, selecting, hiring, orienting, or even training the employees. Merely issue them uniforms and send them off to clean rooms. Some employers may even be willing to relax their responsibilities regarding employment law such as immigration and naturalization requirements. Management should never forget that once a contracted employee dons a company uniform, the guest believes that person is an employee of the hotel. The guest also believes the hotel has made every reasonable effort to screen that person in the hiring process to ensure that he or she is of good moral character, who has the best interest of the guest at heart.

Unfortunately, there have been several incidents in which the outsourced employees did not quite have the best interest of the guest in their hearts. There have been more than a few cases in which outsourced workers were wanted felons who inflicted considerable bodily harm on guests during the performance of their duties. A number of these incidents have resulted in lawsuits, with awards against the hotel in the millions of dollars.

3

Effective Housekeeping

Cleanliness, punctuality, order, and method, are essentials in the character of a good housekeeper. Without the first, no household can be said to be well managed. The second is equally all-important; for those who are under the housekeeper will take their "cue" from her; and in the same proportion as punctuality governs her movements, so will it theirs. Order, again, is indispensable; for by it we wish to be understood that "there should be a place for everything, and everything in its place."

Method, too, is most necessary; for when the work is properly contrived, and each part arranged in regular succession, it will be done more quickly and more effectually. The housekeeper must consider herself as the immediate representative of her mistress, and bring, to the management of the household, all those qualities of honesty, industry, and vigilance, in the same degree as if she were at the head of her own family. Constantly on the watch to detect any wrong-doing on the part of any of the domestics, she will overlook all that goes on in the house, and will see that every department is thoroughly attended to, and that the servants are comfortable, at the same time that their various duties are properly performed.

A necessary qualification for a housekeeper is, that she should thoroughly understand accounts. She will have to write in her books an accurate registry of all sums paid for any and every purpose, all the current expenses of the house, tradesmen's bills, and other extraneous matter. Under the head of the Mistress, a housekeeper's accounts should be periodically balanced, and examined by the head of the house. Nothing tends more to the satisfaction of both employer and employed, than this arrangement. "Short reckonings make long friends," stands good in this case, as in others.

It will be found an excellent plan to take an account of every article which comes into the house connected with housekeeping, and is not paid for at the time. The book containing these entries can then be compared with the bills sent in by the various tradesmen, so that any discrepancy can be inquired into and set right. An intelligent housekeeper will, by this means, too, be better able to judge of the average consumption of each article by the household; and if that quantity be, at any time, exceeded, the cause may be discovered and rectified, if it proceed from waste or carelessness.

Although in the department of the cook, the housekeeper does not generally much interfere, yet it is necessary that she should possess a good knowledge of the culinary art, as, in many instances, it may be requisite for her to take the superintendence of the kitchen. As a rule, it may be stated, that the housekeeper, in those establishments where there is no house steward or man cook, undertakes the preparation of the confectionary, attends to the preserving and pickling of fruits and vegetables; and, in a general way, to the more difficult branches of the art of cookery.

Much of these arrangements will depend, however, on the qualifications of the cook; for instance, if she be an able artiste, there will be but little necessity for the housekeeper to interfere, except in the already noticed articles of confectionary, etc. On the contrary, if the cook be not so clever an adept in her art, then it will be requisite for the housekeeper to give more of her attention to the business of the kitchen, than in the former case. It will be one of the duties of the housekeeper to attend to the marketing, in the absence of either a house steward or man cook.

The daily duties of a housekeeper are regulated, in a great measure, by the extent of the establishment she superintends. She should, however, rise early, and see that all the domestics are duly performing their work, and that everything is progressing satisfactorily for the preparation of the breakfast for the household and family.

After breakfast, which, in large establishments, she will take in the "housekeeper's room" with the lady's-maid, butler, and valet, and where they will be waited on by the still-room maid, she will, on various days set apart for each purpose, carefully examine the household linen, with a view to its being repaired, or to a further quantity being put in hand to be made; she will also see that the furniture throughout the house is well rubbed and polished; and will, besides, attend to all the necessary details of marketing and ordering goods from the tradesmen.

The housekeeper's room is generally made use of by the lady's-maid, butler, and valet, who take there their breakfast, tea, and supper. The lady's-maid will also use this apartment as a sitting-room, when not engaged with her lady, or with some other duties, which would call her elsewhere. In different establishments, according to their size and the rank of the family, different rules of course prevail. For instance, in the mansions of those of very high rank, and where there is a house steward, there are two distinct tables kept, one in the steward's room for the principal members of the household, the other in the servants' hall, for the other domestics.

At the steward's dinner-table, the steward and housekeeper preside; and here, also, are present the lady's-maid, butler, valet, and head gardener. Should any visitors be staying with the family, their servants, generally the valet and lady's-maid, will be admitted to the steward's table. After dinner, the housekeeper, having seen that all the members of the establishment have regularly returned to their various duties, and that all the departments of the household are in proper working order, will have many important matters claiming her attention.

She will, possibly, have to give the finishing touch to some article of confectionary, or be occupied with some of the more elaborate processes of the still-room. There may also be the dessert to arrange, ice-creams to make; and all these employments call for no ordinary degree of care, taste, and attention. The still-room was formerly much more in vogue than at present; for in days of "auld lang syne," the still was in constant requisition for the supply of sweet-flavoured waters for the purposes of cookery, scents and aromatic substances used in the preparation of the toilet, and cordials in cases of accidents and illness.

There are some establishments, however, in which distillation is still carried on, and in these, the still-room maid has her old duties to perform. In a general way, however, this domestic is immediately concerned with the housekeeper. For the latter she lights the fire, dusts her room, prepares the breakfast-table, and waits at the different meals taken in the housekeeper's room. A still-room maid may learn a very great deal of useful knowledge from her intimate connection with the housekeeper, and if she be active and intelligent, may soon fit herself for a better position in the household.

In the evening, the housekeeper will often busy herself with the necessary preparations for the next day's duties. Numberless small, but still important arrangements, will have to be made, so that everything may move smoothly. At times, perhaps, attention will have to be paid to the breaking of lump-sugar, the stoning of raisins, the washing, cleansing, and drying of currants, &c.

The evening, too, is the best time for setting right her account of the expenditure, and duly writing a statement of moneys received and paid, and also for making memoranda of any articles she may require for her storeroom or other departments. Periodically, at some convenient time — for instance, quarterly or half-yearly, it is a good plan for the housekeeper to make an inventory of everything she has under her care, and compare this with the lists of a former period; she will then be able to furnish a statement, if necessary, of the articles which, on account of time, breakage, loss, or other causes, it has been necessary to replace or replenish.

Like "Caesar's wife," she should be "above suspicion," and her honesty and sobriety unquestionable; for there are many temptations to which she is exposed. In a physical point of view, a housekeeper should be healthy and strong, and be particularly clean in her person, and her hands, although they may show a degree of roughness, from the nature of some of her employments, yet should have a nice inviting appearance.

In her dealings with the various tradesmen, and in her behaviour to the domestics under her, the demeanour and conduct of the housekeeper should be such as, in neither case, to diminish, by an undue familiarity, her authority or influence. As, in the winter months, servants have much more to do, in consequence of the necessity there is to attend to the number of fires throughout the household, not much more than the ordinary every-day work can be attempted.

In the summer, and when the absence of fires gives the domestics more leisure, then any extra work that is required, can be more easily performed. The spring is the usual period set apart for house-cleaning, and removing all the dust and dirt, which will necessarily, with the best of housewives, accumulate during the winter months, from the smoke of the coal, oil, gas, &c. This season is also well adapted for washing and bleaching linen, &c., as, the weather, not being then too hot for the exertions necessary in washing counterpanes, blankets, and heavy things in general, the work is better and more easily done than in the intense heats of July, which month some recommend for these purposes.

Winter curtains should be taken down, and replaced by the summer white ones; and furs and woollen cloths also carefully laid by. The former should be well shaken and brushed, and then pinned upon paper or linen, with camphor to preserve them from the moths. Furs, &c., will be preserved in the same way. Included, under the general description of house-cleaning, must be understood, turning out all the nooks and corners of drawers, cupboards, lumber-rooms, lofts, &c., with a view of getting rid of all unnecessary articles, which only create dirt and attract vermin; sweeping of chimneys, taking up carpets, painting and whitewashing the kitchen and offices, papering rooms, when needed, and, generally speaking, the house putting on, with the approaching summer, a bright appearance, and a new face, in unison with nature.

Oranges now should be preserved, and orange wine made. The summer will be found, as mentioned above, in consequence of the diminution of labour for the domestics, the best period for examining and repairing household linen, and for "putting to rights" all those articles which have received a large share of wear and tear during the dark winter days. In direct reference to this matter, that sheets should be turned "sides to middle" before they are allowed to get very thin. Otherwise, patching, which is uneconomical from the time it consumes, and is unsightly in point of appearance, will have to be resorted to.

In June and July, gooseberries, currants, raspberries, strawberries, and other summer fruits, should be preserved, and jams and jellies made. In July, too, the making of walnut ketchup should be attended to, as the green walnuts will be approaching perfection for this purpose. Mixed pickles may also be now made, and it will be found a good plan to have ready a jar of pickle-juice, into which to put occasionally some young French beans, cauliflowers, etc.

In the early autumn, plums of various kinds are to be bottled and preserved, and jams and jellies made. A little later, tomato sauce, a most useful article to have by you, may be prepared; a supply of apples laid in, if you have a place to keep them, as also a few keeping pears and filberts. Endeavour to keep also a large vegetable marrow it will be found delicious in the winter.

In October and November, it will be necessary to prepare for the cold weather, and get ready the winter clothing for the various members of the family. The white summer curtains will now be carefully put away, the fireplaces, grates, and chimneys looked to, and the House put in a thorough state of repair, so that no "loose tile" may, at a future day, interfere with your comfort, and extract something considerable from your pocket.

In December, the principal household duty lies in preparing for the creature comforts of those near and dear to us, so as to meet old Christmas with a happy face, a contented mind, and a full larder; and in stoning the plums, washing the currants, cutting the citron, beating the eggs, and mixing the pudding, a housewife is not unworthily greeting the genial season of all good things.

4

Role of Housekeepers

Executive housekeepers and the housekeeping staff ensure that hotel rooms, hospital rooms, and rooms and public areas in schools, colleges, and universities are neat, clean, and attractive. Executive housekeepers (ex'e-cu-tive 'house-keep-ers) oversee staff who keep hotels, hospitals, educational institutions, and similar establishments clean, orderly, and attractive.

High standards for cleanliness and efficient housekeeping are important for the success of these institutions. Hospital rooms must be clean for the health, safety, and well-being of the patients. Executive housekeepers hire, train, and supervise others to help them in this task. In small organizations, they may be in charge of a staff of two or three workers. In large institutions, they may supervise a hundred people or more.

They may work in motels, resorts, clubs, condominiums, hospitals, nursing homes, retirement homes, or residence halls in schools and colleges. Most often, they work in large hotels. In very large hotels executive housekeepers, also called directors of housekeeping, spend most of their time on administrative duties. They organize housekeeping departments, establish cleaning standards and procedures, and set up work schedules.

They meet with the directors of other departments in the hotel to coordinate activities and schedules. Executive housekeepers hire, train, and supervise their assistants, room attendants, hall cleaners, house persons, laundry workers, linen room workers, wall and window washers, seamstresses, upholsterers, painters, cabinetmakers, and other housekeeping workers skilled in repair and maintenance.

They organize and direct training programs for the staff. They resolve personnel issues and evaluate employee performance. Executive housekeepers inspect rooms for cleanliness and check on other housekeeping tasks to make sure that workers are following proper procedures. They make sure that the work of the housekeeping department falls within the established standards of quality for the hotel.

In some establishments executive housekeepers supervise the staff who set up rooms for conventions, banquets, exhibits, and other programs. Executive housekeepers may be in charge of ordering housekeeping supplies and equipment. They may help in the selection and purchase of new furniture. Some executive housekeepers work with interior decorators to develop new decorating schemes for rooms and public areas.

The housekeeping staff tells the executive housekeeper about damage and equipment that needs repair. Executive housekeepers conduct their own inspections and make recommendations on the relocation of equipment and the use of space. They also develop procedures on how to inform the engineering/ maintenance department when its services are needed. They keep records on personnel, payroll, expenses, and housekeeping activities.

They keep management informed about repair work, improvements, personnel difficulties, and expenditures.

They submit a yearly budget for review and approval. In small or medium-sized hotels and motels executive housekeepers may share cleaning chores with the staff. Executive housekeepers who work in small institutions may also be in charge of other operations such as maintenance and ordering food. Housekeepers in hospitals make sure that patients have safe, clean rooms.

They follow strict procedures for cleanliness and sanitation to prevent the spread of infection and disease. They develop education programs for the staff and teach them how to handle contaminated wastes safely. They teach them safety techniques and the correct way to use supplies and equipment. Staff development is important, and executive housekeepers make sure staff education programs are ongoing.

As a rule, working conditions are very good. Executive housekeepers work in clean, attractive, comfortable buildings. Although they usually have their own office, they spend a good part of their time in other parts of the establishment. They may be on their feet most of the day.

Hours and Earnings

Most executive housekeepers work forty to forty-eight hours a week. Housekeepers in resort hotels or motels may work longer hours during the tourist season. Executive housekeepers who live in the hotel have regular hours, but they may be on call at any time. Executive housekeepers in hospitals, schools, and other institutions usually work forty hours a week.

Salaries depend on the experience and education of the housekeeper and the size and location of the establishment that employs them. According to the Bureau of Labor Statistics, in 2000, executive housekeepers averaged $27,830 a year. Salaries ranged from $7.80 to

$20.60 an hour, or $16,220 to $42,850 a year. Some hotels may offer executive housekeepers and their families room and board and use of hotel services. Other benefits are paid vacations, sick leave, hospital insurance, and tuition assistance for continuing education.

Education and Training

At one time the job of executive housekeeper went to the person in the housekeeping department with the most experience or seniority. Today, many executive housekeepers have a college degree or have taken advanced courses in business and management. Executive housekeepers will have better employment opportunities if they have at least a two-year college degree or have taken some advanced courses in hospitality.

They should have a basic knowledge of accounting to keep records and to prepare budgets and reports. A knowledge of labor laws and safety regulations is important. Executive housekeepers may also find it helpful to study sociology, psychology, economics, personnel management and human relations, and communications. Purchasing, interior design, maintenance and inventory control, basic computer skills, and rules and procedures for sanitation and health may be beneficial.

Universities, community colleges, and vocational schools offer programs that prepare students for institutional housekeeping. These schools may also offer continuing education courses for those already in the field. The Educational Institute of the American Hotel & Lodging Association, and the International Executive Housekeepers Association, offer home-study courses and certification programs for executive housekeepers.

High school students should take business courses, along with courses in general science and chemistry. Many students get a head start in housekeeping careers by working part time for hospitals, hotels, motels, resorts, and summer camps.

Professional Societies

Many executive housekeepers belong to the International Executive Housekeepers Association (IEHA). IEHA is a professional organization with over 6,000 members who work in commercial, institutional, or industrial settings. The International Executive Housekeepers Association has established educational standards for the profession and sponsors certificate and college degree programs.

IEHA also offers numerous self-study courses. Executive housekeepers may also belong to the American Hotel & Lodging Association (AH&LA). AH&LA is a professional organization with over 13,000 property members who work in the hotel and lodging industry. AH&LA also offers educational services and a certification program for executive housekeepers.

Personal Qualifications

Executive housekeepers should be intelligent, poised, and friendly. They should be flexible, patient, and have a sense of humor. They should have good organizational skills and should be able to manage several tasks at once. Executive housekeepers should be able to communicate well with management, staff, the public, and suppliers. Occupations can be adapted for workers with disabilities.

Persons should contact their school or employment counselors, their state office of vocational rehabilitation, or their state department of labor to explore fully their individual needs and requirements as well as the requirements of the occupation.

Executive housekeepers work in hotels, motels, condominiums, and clubs. Others work in hospitals, nursing homes, and health-care centers. Some work on college campuses or in schools. Many of the best jobs are in large cities and their suburbs. A growing number of resort hotels and motels in less populated places also offer excellent opportunities.

According to the Bureau of Labor Statistics, the number of jobs for executive housekeepers is expected to increase about as fast as the average for all occupations. The hospitality industry is enjoying moderate growth in the twenty-first century. Some developers are building new hotels and resorts. These establishments may create opportunities for executive housekeepers who are new to the field. The demand may be offset by the limited number of positions available-since each hotel requires only one executive housekeeper.

Economy hotel chains often hire one executive housekeeper to oversee several hotels in the chain. Most jobs will open as workers retire or find work in other occupations. Some large establishments require prospective executive housekeepers to have a college degree in hotel and restaurant management. Others may hire experienced workers who have taken courses in the field. Job seekers may start as floor supervisors, executive assistants, or assistant heads of housekeeping departments.

They learn housekeeping procedures and policies and gain experience managing a staff. In time they may take over the management of the housekeeping department during the late afternoon or evening shift. Smaller hotels and motels may hire executive housekeepers who lack a formal education in the hospitality field but have worked their way up through the ranks.

However, even in these small institutions, the trend has been to look for candidates who have taken some hospitality or business courses. Job seekers may find opportunities at newly built hotels, resorts, hospitals, nursing homes, or other establishments. The International Executive Housekeepers Association maintains a referral service for job seekers and for employers looking for candidates.

Since executive housekeepers already hold the top position in their profession, further advancement may be limited. In many small establishments executive housekeepers may become assistant managers. With more education and experience they may be promoted to become managers. Executive housekeepers in many institutions are considered part of the top management team.

Executive housekeepers in chain properties or franchise establishments can advance to positions in corporate executive housekeeping. They may become inspectors, consultants, or specialists in the process of opening new branches. Housekeepers in hospitals and other institutions may advance by taking similar jobs in larger establishments with higher pay. They may become general service managers or administrators in hotels or other institutions. Some housekeeping department heads may become hospital administrators.

5

Responsibilities of Butler, Footman and Valet

Responsibilities of Butler

The domestic duties of the butler are to bring in the eatables at breakfast, and wait upon the family at that meal, assisted by the footman, and see to the cleanliness of everything at table. On taking away, he removes the tray with the china and plate, for which he is responsible. At luncheon, he arranges the meal, and waits unassisted, the footman being now engaged in other duties.

At dinner, he places the silver and plated articles on the table, sees that everything is in its place, and rectifies what is wrong. He carries in the first dish, and announces in the drawing-room that dinner is on the table, and respectfully stands by the door until the company are seated, when he takes his place behind his master's chair on the left, to remove the covers, handing them to the other attendants to carry out. After the first course of plates is supplied, his place is at the sideboard to serve the wines, but only when called on.

The first course ended, he rings the cook's bell, and hands the dishes from the table to the other servants to carry away, receiving from them the second course, which he places on the table, removing the covers as before, and again taking his place at the sideboard. At dessert, the slips being removed, the butler receives the dessert from the other servants, and arranges it on the table, with plates and glasses, and then takes his place behind his master's chair to hand the wines and ices, while the footman stands behind his mistress for the same purpose, the other attendants leaving the room.

Where the old-fashioned practice of having the dessert on the polished table, without any cloth, is still adhered to, the butler should rub off any marks made by the hot dishes before arranging the dessert. Before dinner, he has satisfied himself that the lamps, candles, or gas-burners are in perfect order, if not lighted, which will usually be the case. Having served every one with their share of the dessert, put the fires in order, and seen the lights are all right, at a signal from his master, he and the footman leave the room.

He now proceeds to the drawing-room, arranges the fireplace, and sees to the lights; he then returns to his pantry, prepared to answer the bell, and attend to the company, while the footman is clearing away and cleaning the plate and glasses. At tea he again attends. At bedtime he appears with the candles; he locks up the plate, secures doors and windows, and sees that all the fires are safe. In addition to these duties, the butler, where only one footman is kept, will be required to perform some of the duties of the valet, to pay bills, and superintend the other servants.

But the real duties of the butler are in the wine-cellar; there he should be competent to advise his master as to the price and quality of the wine to be laid in; "fine," bottle, cork, and seal it, and place it in the binns. Brewing, racking, and bottling malt liquors, belong to his office, as well as their distribution. These and other drinkables are brought from the cellar every day by his own hands, except where an under-butler is kept; and a careful entry of every bottle used, entered in the cellar-book; so that the book should always show the contents of the cellar. The office of butler is thus one of very great trust in a household. Here, as elsewhere, honesty is the best policy: the butler should make it his business to understand the proper treatment of the different wines under his charge, which he can easily do from the wine-merchant, and faithfully attend to it; his own reputation will soon compensate for the absence of bribes from unprincipled wine-merchants, if he serves a generous and hospitable master.

Nothing spreads more rapidly in society than the reputation of a good wine-cellar, and all that is required is wines well chosen and well cared for; and this a little knowledge, carefully applied, will soon supply. The butler, has charge of the contents of the cellars, and it is his duty to keep them in a proper condition, to fine down wine in wood, bottle it off, and store it away in places suited to the sorts. Where wine comes into the cellar ready bottled, it is usual to return the same number of empty bottles; the butler has not, in this case, the same inducements to keep the bottles of the different sorts separated; but where the wine is bottled in the house, he will find his account, not only in keeping them separate, but in rinsing them well, and even washing them with clean water as soon as they are empty.

There are various modes of fining wine: isinglass, gelatine, and gum Arabic are all used for the purpose. Whichever of these articles is used, the process is always the same. Supposing eggs to be used,– Draw a gallon or so of the wine, and mix one quart of it with the whites of four eggs, by stirring it with a whisk; afterwards, when thoroughly mixed, pour it back into the cask through the bunghole, and stir up the whole cask, in a rotatory direction, with a clean split stick inserted through the bunghole. Having stirred it sufficiently, pour in the remainder of the wine drawn off, until the cask is full; then stir again, skimming off the bubbles that rise to the surface.

When thoroughly mixed by stirring, close the bunghole, and leave it to stand for three or four days. This quantity of clarified wine will fine thirteen dozen of port or sherry. The other clearing ingredients are applied in the same manner, the material being cut into small pieces, and dissolved in the quart of wine, and the cask stirred in the same manner.

Having thoroughly washed and dried the bottles, supposing they have been before used for the same kind of wine, provide corks, which will be improved by being slightly boiled, or at least steeped in hot water,– a wooden hammer or mallet, a bottling-boot, and a squeezer for the corks. Bore a hole in the lower part of the cask with a gimlet, receiving the liquid stream which follows in the bottle and filterer, which is placed in a tub or basin. This operation is best performed by two persons, one to draw the wine, the other to cork the bottles. The drawer is to see that the bottles are up to the mark, but not too full, the bottle being placed in a clean tub to prevent waste.

The corking-boot is buckled by a strap to the knee, the bottle placed in it, and the cork, after being squeezed in the press, driven in by a flat wooden mallet. As the wine draws near to the bottom of the cask, a thick piece of muslin is placed in the strainer, to prevent the viscous grounds from passing into the bottle. Having carefully counted the bottles, they are stored away in their respective binns, a layer of sand or sawdust being placed under the first tier, and another over it; a second tier is laid over this, protected by a lath, the head of the second being laid to the bottom of the first; over this another bed of sawdust is laid, not too thick, another lath; and so on till the binn is filled.

Wine so laid in will be ready for use according to its quality and age. Port wine, old in the wood, will be ready to drink in five or six months; but if it is a fruity wine, it will improve every year. Sherry, if of good quality, will be fit to drink as soon as the "sickness" ceases, and will also improve; but the cellar must be kept at a perfectly steady temperature, neither too hot nor too cold, but about 55° or 60°, and absolutely free from draughts of cold air.

Responsibilities of Footman

Where a single footman, or odd man, is the only male servant, then, whatever his ostensible position, he is required to make himself generally useful. He has to clean the knives and shoes, the furniture, the plate; answer the visitors who call, the drawing-room and parlour bells; and do all the errands. His life is no sinecure; and a methodical arrangement of his time will be necessary, in order to perform his many duties with any satisfaction to himself or his master.

The footman only finds himself in stockings, shoes, and washing. Where silk stockings, or other extra articles of linen are worn, they are found by the family, as well as his livery, a working dress, consisting of a pair of overalls, a waistcoat, a fustian jacket, with a white or jean one for times when he is liable to be called to answer the door or wait at breakfast; and, on quitting his service, he is expected to leave behind him any livery had within six months.

The footman is expected to rise early, in order to get through all his dirty work before the family are stirring. Boots and shoes, and knives and forks, should be cleaned, lamps in use trimmed, his master's clothes brushed, the furniture rubbed over; so that he may put aside his working dress, tidy himself, and appear in a clean jean jacket to lay the cloth and prepare breakfast for the family.

The boot-cleaning process: three good brushes and good blacking must be provided; one of the brushes hard, to brush off the mud; the other soft, to lay on the blacking; the third of a medium hardness, for polishing; and each should be kept for its particular use. The blacking should be kept corked up, except when in use, and applied to the brush with a sponge tied to a stick, which, when put away, rests in a notch cut in the cork.

When boots come in very muddy, it is a good practice to wash off the mud, and wipe them dry with a sponge; then leave them to dry very gradually on their sides, taking care they are not placed near the fire, or scorched. Much delicacy of treatment is required in cleaning ladies' boots, so as to make the leather look well-polished, and the upper part retain a fresh appearance, with the lining free from hand-marks, which are very offensive to a lady of refined tastes.

Patent leather boots require to be wiped with a wet sponge, and afterwards with a soft dry cloth, and occasionally with a soft cloth and sweet oil, blacking and polishing the edge of the soles in the usual way, but so as not to cover the patent polish with blacking. A little milk may also be used with very good effect for patent leather boots. Top boots are still occasionally worn by gentlemen. While cleaning the lower part in the usual manner, protect the tops, by inserting a cloth or brown paper under the edges and bringing it over them.

In cleaning the tops, let the covering fall down over the boot; wash the tops clean with soap and flannel, and rub out any spots with pumice-stone. If the tops are to be whiter, dissolve an ounce of oxalic acid and half an ounce of pumice-stone in a pint of soft water; if a brown colour is intended, mix an ounce of muriatic acid, half an ounce of alum, half an ounce of gum Arabic, and half an ounce of spirit of lavender, in a pint and a half of skimmed milk "turned."

These mixtures apply by means of a sponge, and polish, when dry, with a rubber made of soft flannel. Knives are now generally cleaned by means of Kent's or Masters's machine, which gives very little trouble, and is very effective; before, however, putting the knives into the machine, it is highly necessary that they be first washed in a little warm (not hot) water, and then thoroughly wiped: if put into the machine with any grease on them, it adheres to the brushes, and consequently renders them unfit to use for the next knives that may be put in.

When this precaution is not taken, the machine must come to pieces, so causing an immense amount of trouble, which may all be avoided by having the knives thoroughly free from grease before using the machine. Brushes are also used for cleaning forks, which facilitate the operation. When knives are so cleaned, see that they are carefully polished, wiped, and with a good edge, the ferules and prongs free from dirt, and place them in the basket with the handles all one way.

Lamp-trimming requires a thorough acquaintance with the mechanism; after that, constant attention to cleanliness, and an occasional entire clearing out with hot water: when this is done, all the parts should be carefully dried before filling again with oil. When lacquered, wipe the lacquered parts with a soft brush and cloth, and wash occasionally with weak soapsuds, wiping carefully afterwards. Brass lamps may be cleaned with oil and rottenstone every day when trimmed.

With bronze, and other ornamental lamps, more care will be required, and soft flannel and oil only used, to prevent the removal of the bronze or enamel. Brass-work, or any metal-work not lacquered, is cleaned by a little oil and rottenstone made into a paste, or with fine emery-powder and oil mixed in the same manner. A small portion of sal ammoniac, beat into a fine powder and moistened with soft water, rubbed over brass ornaments, and heated over a charcoal fire, and rubbed dry with bran or whitening, will give to brass-work the brilliancy of gold.

In trimming moderator lamps, let the wick be cut evenly all round; as, if left higher in one place than it is in another, it will cause it to smoke and burn badly. The lamp should then be filled with oil from a feeder, and afterwards well wiped with a cloth or rag kept for the purpose. If it can be avoided, never wash the chimneys of a lamp, as it causes them to crack when they become hot. Small sticks, covered with wash-leather pads, are the best things to use for cleaning the glasses inside, and a clean duster for polishing the outside.

The globe of a moderator lamp should be occasionally washed in warm soap-and-water, then well rinsed in cold water, and either wiped dry or left to drain. Where candle-lamps are used, take out the springs occasionally, and free them well from the grease that adheres to them. French polish, so universally applied to furniture, is easily kept in condition by dusting and rubbing with a soft cloth, or a rubber of old silk; but dining-tables can only be kept in order by hard rubbing, or rather by quick rubbing, which warms the wood and removes all spots.

Brushing clothes is a very simple but very necessary operation. Fine cloths require to be brushed lightly, and with rather a soft brush, except where mud is to be removed, when a hard one is necessary, being previously beaten lightly to dislodge the dirt. Lay the garment on a table, and brush it in the direction of the nap. Having brushed it properly, turn the sleeves back to the collar, so that the folds may come at the elbow-joints; next turn the lappels or sides back over the folded sleeves; then lay the skirts over level with the collar, so that the crease may fall about the centre, and double one half over the other, so as the fold comes in the centre of the back.

Having got through his dirty work, the single footman has now to clean himself and prepare the breakfast. He lays the cloth on the table; over it the breakfast-cloth, and sets the breakfast things in order, and then proceeds to wait upon his master, if he has any of the duties of a valet to perform. Where a valet is not kept, a portion of his duties falls to the footman's share,–brushing the clothes among others. When the hat is silk, it requires brushing every day with a soft brush; after rain, it requires wiping the way of the nap before drying, and, when nearly dry, brushing with the soft brush and with the hat-stick in it.

If the footman is required to perform any part of a valet's duties, he will have to see that the housemaid lights a fire in the dressing-room in due time; that the room is dusted and cleaned; that the washhand-ewer is filled with soft water; and that the bath, whether hot or cold, is ready when required; that towels are at hand; that hair-brushes and combs are properly cleansed, and in their places; that hot water is ready at the hour ordered; the dressing-gown and slippers in their place, the clean linen aired, and the clothes to be worn for the day in their proper places.

After the master has dressed, it will be the footman's duty to restore everything to its place properly cleansed and dry, and the whole restored to order. At breakfast, when there is no butler, the footman carries up the tea-urn, and, assisted by the housemaid, he waits during breakfast. Breakfast over, he removes the tray and other things off the table, folds up the breakfast-cloth, and sets the room in order, by sweeping up all crumbs, shaking the cloth, and laying it on the table again, making up the fire, and sweeping up the hearth.

At luncheon-time nearly the same routine is observed, except where the footman is either out with the carriage or away on other business, when, in the absence of any butler, the housemaid must assist. For dinner, the footman lays the cloth, taking care that the table is not too near the fire, if there is one, and that passage-room is left. A tablecloth should be laid without a wrinkle; and this requires two persons: over this the slips are laid, which are usually removed preparatory to placing dessert on the table. He prepares knives, forks, and glasses, with five or six plates for each person.

This done, he places chairs enough for the party, distributing them equally on each side of the table, and opposite to each a napkin neatly folded, within it a piece of bread or small roll, and a knife on the right side of each plate, a fork on the left, and a carving-knife and fork at the top and bottom of the table, outside the others, with the rests opposite to them, and a gravy-spoon beside the knife.

The fish-slice should be at the top, where the lady of the house, with the assistance of the gentleman next to her, divides the fish, and the soup-ladle at the bottom: it is sometimes usual to add a dessert-knife and fork; at the same time, on the right side also of each plate, put a wine-glass for as many kinds of wine as it is intended to hand round, and a finger-glass or glass-cooler about four inches from the edge. The latter are frequently put on the table with the dessert. About half an hour before dinner, he rings the dinner-bell, where that is the practice, and occupies himself with carrying up everything he is likely to require.

At the expiration of the time, having communicated with the cook, he rings the real dinner-bell, and proceeds to take it up with such assistance as he can obtain. Having ascertained that all is in order, that his own dress is clean and presentable, and his white cotton gloves are without a stain, he announces in the drawing-room that dinner is served, and stands respectfully by the door until the company are seated: he places himself on the left, behind his master, who is to distribute the soup; where soup and fish are served together, his place will be at his mistress's left hand; but he must be on the alert to see that whoever is assisting him, whether male or female, are at their posts. If any of the guests has brought his own servant with him, his place is behind his master's chair, rendering such assistance to others as he can, while attending to his master's wants throughout the dinner, so that every guest has what he requires.

This necessitates both activity and intelligence, and should be done without bustle, without asking any questions, except where it is the custom of the house to hand round dishes or wine, when it will be necessary to mention, in a quiet and unobtrusive manner, the dish or wine you present. Salt-cellars should be placed on the table in number sufficient for the guests, so that each may help themselves, or, at least, their immediate neighbours.

Special Duties in the Time of Dinner

In some hotels and houses the table is laid out with plate and glass, and ornamented with flowers, the dessert only being placed on the table, the dinner itself being placed on the sideboard, and handed round in succession, in courses of soup, fish, entries, meat, game, and sweets. This is not only elegant but economical, as fewer dishes are required, the symmetry of the table being made up with the ornaments and dessert.

The various dishes are also handed round when hot; but it involves additional and superior attendance, as the wines are also handed round; and unless the servants are very active and intelligent, many blunders are likely to be made. While attentive to all, the footman should be obtrusive to none; he should give nothing but on a waiter, and always hand it with the left hand and on the left side of the person he serves, and hold it so that the guest may take it with ease.

In lifting dishes from the table, he should use both hands, and remove them with care, so that nothing is spilt on the table-cloth or on the dresses of the guests. Masters as well as servants sometimes make mistakes; but it is not expected that a servant will correct any omissions, even if he should have time to notice them, although with the best intentions: thus it would not be correct, for instance, if he observed that his master took wine with the ladies all round, as some gentlemen still continue to do, but stopped at some one:–

To nudge him on the shoulder and say, as was done by the servant of a Scottish gentleman, "What ails you at her in the green gown?" It will be better to leave the lady unnoticed than for the servant thus to turn his master into ridicule. During dinner each person's knife, fork, plate, and spoon should be changed as soon as he has done with it; the vegetables and sauces belonging to the different dishes presented without remark to the guests; and the footman should tread lightly in moving round, and, if possible, should bear in mind, if there is a wit or humorist of the party, whose good things keep the table in a roar, that they are not expected to reach his ears.

In opening wine, let it be done quietly, and without shaking the bottle; if crusted, let it be inclined to the crusted side, and decanted while in that position. In opening champagne, it is not necessary to discharge it with a pop; properly cooled, the cork is easily extracted without an explosion; when the cork is out, the mouth of the bottle should be wiped with the napkin over the footman's arm.

At the end of the first course, notice is conveyed to the cook, who is waiting to send up the second, which is introduced in the same way as before; the attendants who remove the fragments, carrying the dishes from the kitchen, and handing them to the footman or butler, whose duty it is to arrange them on the table. After dinner, the dessert-glasses and wines are placed on the table by the footman, who places himself behind his master's chair, to supply wine and hand round the ices and other refreshments, all other servants leaving the room.

As soon as the drawing-room bell rings for tea, the footman enters with the tray, which has been previously prepared; hands the tray round to the company, with cream and sugar, the tea and coffee being generally poured out, while another attendant hands cakes, toast, or biscuits. If it is an ordinary family party, where this social meal is prepared by the mistress, he carries the urn or kettle, as the case may be; hands round the toast, or such other eatable as may be required, removing the whole in the same manner when tea is over.

After each meal, the footman's place is in his pantry: here perfect order should prevail – a place for everything and everything in its place. A sink, with hot and cold water laid on, is very desirable, – cold absolutely necessary. Wooden bowls or tubs of sufficient capacity are required, one for hot and another for cold water. Have the bowl three parts full of clean hot water; in this wash all plate and plated articles which are greasy, wiping them before cleaning with the brush.

The footman in small families, where only one man is kept, has many of the duties of the upper servants to perform as well as his own, and more constant occupation; he will also have the arrangement of his time more immediately under his own control, and he will do well to reduce it to a methodical division. All his rough work should be done before breakfast is ready, when he must appear clean, and in a presentable state. After breakfast, when everything belonging to his pantry is cleaned and put in its place, the furniture in the dining and drawing rooms requires rubbing.

Towards noon, the parlour luncheon is to be prepared; and he must be at his mistress's disposal to go out with the carriage, or follow her if she walks out. Glass is a beautiful and most fragile article: hence it requires great care in washing. A perfectly clean wooden bowl is best for this operation, one for moderately hot and another for cold water. Wash the glasses well in the first and rinse them in the second, and turn them down on a linen cloth folded two or three times, to drain for a few minutes.

When sufficiently drained, wipe them with a cloth and polish with a finer one, doing so tenderly and carefully. Accidents will happen; but nothing discredits a servant in the drawing-room more than continual reports of breakages, which, of course, must reach that region. Decanters and water-jugs require still more tender treatment in cleaning, inasmuch as they are more costly to replace.

Fill them about two-thirds with hot but not boiling water, and put in a few pieces of well-soaped brown paper; leave them thus for two or three hours; then shake the water up and down in the decanters; empty this out, rinse them well with clean cold water, and put them in a rack to drain. When dry, polish them outside and inside, as far as possible, with a fine cloth. To remove the crust of port or other wines, add a little muriatic acid to the water, and let it remain for some time.

When required to go out with the carriage, it is the footman's duty to see that it has come to the door perfectly clean, and that the glasses, and sashes, and linings, are free from dust. In receiving messages at the carriage door, he should turn his ear to the speaker, so as to comprehend what is said, in order that he may give his directions to the coachman clearly. When the house he is to call at is reached, he should knock, and return to the carriage for orders. In closing the door upon the family, he should see that the handle is securely turned, and that no part of the ladies' dress is shut in.

It is the footman's duty to carry messages or letters for his master or mistress to their friends, to the post, or to the tradespeople; and nothing is more important than dispatch and exactness in doing so, although writing even the simplest message is now the ordinary and very proper practice. Dean Swift, among his other quaint directions, all of which are to be read by contraries, recommends a perusal of all such epistles, in order that you may be the more able to fulfil your duty to your master. An old lady of Forfarshire had one of those odd old Caleb Balderston sort of servants, who construed the Dean of St. Patrick more literally.

On one occasion, when dispatch was of some importance, knowing his inquiring nature, she called her Scotch Paul Pry to her, opened the note, and read it to him herself, saying, "Now, Andrew, you ken a' aboot it, and needna' stop to open and read it, but just take it at once." Probably most of the notes you are expected to carry might, with equal harmlessness, be communicated to you; but it will be better not to take so lively an interest in your mistress's affairs.

Politeness and civility to visitors is one of the things masters and mistresses have a right to expect, and should exact rigorously. When visitors present themselves, the servant charged with the duty of opening the door will open it promptly, and answer, without hesitation, if the family are "not at home," or "engaged;" which generally means the same thing, and might be oftener used with advantage to morals. On the contrary, if he has no such orders, he will answer affirmatively, open the door wide to admit them, and precede them to open the door of the drawing-room.

If the family are not there, he will place chairs for them, open the blinds (if the room is too dark), and intimate civilly that he goes to inform his mistress. If the lady is in her drawing-room, he announces the name of the visitors, having previously acquainted himself with it. In this part of his duty it is necessary to be very careful to repeat the names correctly; mispronouncing names is very apt to give offence, and leads sometimes to other disagreeables. The writer was once initiated into some of the secrets on the "other side" of a legal affair in which he took an interest, before he could correct a mistake made by the servant in announcing him.

When the visitor is departing, the servant should be at hand, ready, when rung for, to open the door; he should open it with a respectful manner, and close it gently when the visitors are fairly beyond the threshold. When several visitors arrive together, he should take care not to mix up the different names together, where they belong to the same family, as Mr., Mrs., and Miss; if they are strangers, he should announce each as distinctly as possible.

Special Duties in the Occasion of Receptions and Parties

The drawing-rooms being prepared, the card-tables laid out with cards and counters, and such other arrangements as are necessary made for the reception of the company, the rooms should be lighted up as the hour appointed approaches. Attendants in the drawing-room, even more than in the dining-room, should move about actively but noiselessly; no creaking of shoes, which is an abomination; watching the lights from time to time, so as to keep up their brilliancy.

But even if the attendant likes a game of cribbage or whist himself, he must not interfere in his master or mistress's game, nor even seem to take an interest in it. A lady who had a footman, and both were fond of a game of cribbage, – John in the kitchen, the lady in her drawing-room. The lady was a giver of evening parties, where she frequently enjoyed her favourite amusement. While handing about the tea and toast, John could not always suppress his disgust at her mistakes.

Responsibilities of Valets

Attendants on the Person.-"No man is a hero to his valet," saith the proverb; and the corollary may run, "No lady is a heroine to her maid." The infirmities of humanity are, perhaps, too numerous and too equally distributed to stand the severe microscopic tests which attendants on the person have opportunities of applying. The valet and waiting-maid are placed near the persons of the master and mistress, receiving orders only from them, dressing them, accompanying them in all their journeys, the confidants and agents of their most unguarded moments, of their most secret habits, and of course subject to their commands,– even to their caprices; they themselves being subject to erring judgment, aggravated by an imperfect education.

All that can be expected from such servants is polite manners, modest demeanour, and a respectful reserve, which are indispensable. To these, good sense, good temper, some self-denial, and consideration for the feelings of others, whether above or below them in the social scale, will be useful qualifications. Their duty leads them to wait on those who are, from sheer wealth, station, and education, more polished, and consequently more susceptible of annoyance; and any vulgar familiarity of manner is opposed to all their notions of self-respect.

Quiet unobtrusive manners, therefore, and a delicate reserve in speaking of their employers, either in praise or blame, is as essential in their absence, as good manners and respectful conduct in their presence. Some of the duties of the valet we have just hinted at in treating of the duties of the footman in a small family. His day commences by seeing that his master's dressing-room is in order; that the housemaid has swept and dusted it properly; that the fire is lighted and burns cheerfully; and some time before his master is expected, he will do well to throw up the sash to admit fresh air, closing it, however, in time to recover the temperature which he knows his master prefers.

It is now his duty to place the body-linen on the horse before the fire, to be aired properly; to lay the trousers intended to be worn, carefully brushed and cleaned, on the back of his master's chair; while the coat and waistcoat, carefully brushed and folded, and the collar cleaned, are laid in their place ready to put on when required. All the articles of the toilet should be in their places, the razors properly set and stropped, and hot water ready for use. Gentlemen generally prefer performing the operation of shaving themselves, but a valet should be prepared to do it if required; and he should, besides, be a good hairdresser.

Shaving over, he has to brush the hair, beard, and moustache, where that appendage is encouraged, arranging the whole simply and gracefully, according to the age and style of countenance. Every fortnight, or three weeks at the utmost, the hair should be cut, and the points of the whiskers trimmed as often as required. A good valet will now present the various articles of the toilet as they are wanted; afterwards, the body-linen, neck-tie, which he will put on, if required, and, afterwards, waistcoat, coat, and boots, in suitable order, and carefully brushed and polished.

Having thus seen his master dressed, if he is about to go out, the valet will hand him his cane, gloves, and hat, the latter well brushed on the outside with a soft brush, and wiped inside with a clean handkerchief, respectfully attend him to the door, and open it for him, and receive his last orders for the day. He now proceeds to put everything in order in the dressing-room, cleans the combs and brushes, and brushes and folds up any clothes that may be left about the room, and puts them away in the drawers.

Gentlemen are sometimes indifferent as to their clothes and appearance; it is the valet's duty, in this case, where his master permits it, to select from the wardrobe such things as are suitable for the occasion, so that he may appear with scrupulous neatness and cleanliness; that his linen and neck-tie, where that is white or coloured, are unsoiled; and where he is not accustomed to change them every day, that the cravat is turned, and even ironed, to remove the crease of the previous fold.

The coat collar,– which where the hair is oily and worn long, is apt to get greasy – should also be examined; a careful valet will correct this by removing the spots day by day as they appear, first by moistening the grease-spots with a little rectified spirits of wine or spirits of hartshorn, which has a renovating effect, and the smell of which soon disappears. The grease is dissolved and removed by gentle scraping. The grease removed, add a little more of the spirit, and rub with a piece of clean cloth; finish by adding a few drops more; rub it with the palm of the hand, in the direction of the grain of the cloth, and it will be clean and glossy as the rest of the garment.

Polish for the boots is an important matter to the valet, and not always to be obtained good by purchase; never so good, perhaps, as he can make for himself after the following recipes:-- Take of ivory-black and treacle each 4 oz., sulphuric acid 1 oz., best olive-oil 2 spoonfuls, best white-wine vinegar 3 half-pints: mix the ivory-black and treacle well in an earthen jar; then add the sulphuric acid, continuing to stir the mixture; next pour in the oil; and, lastly, add the vinegar, stirring it in by degrees, until thoroughly incorporated.

Another polish is made by mixing 1 oz. each of pounded galls and logwood-chips, and 3 lbs. of red French vine (ordinaire). Boil together till the liquid is reduced to half the quantity, and pour it off through a strainer. Now take 1/2 lb. each of pounded gum-arabic and lump-sugar,

1 oz. of green copperas, and 3 lbs. of brandy. Dissolve the gum-arabic in the preceding decoction, and add the sugar and copperas: when all is dissolved and mixed together, stir in the brandy, mixing it smoothly. This mixture will yield 5 or 6 lbs. of a very superior polishing paste for boots and shoes.

It is, perhaps, unnecessary to add, that having discharged all the commissions intrusted to him by his master, such as conveying notes or messages to friends, or the tradesmen, all of which he should punctually and promptly attend to, it is his duty to be in waiting when his master returns home to dress for dinner, or for any other occasion, and to have all things prepared for this second dressing. Previous to this, he brings under his notice the cards of visitors who may have called, delivers the messages be may have received for him, and otherwise acquits himself of the morning's commissions, and receives his orders for the remainder of the day.

The routine of his evening duty is to have the dressing-room and study, where there is a separate one, arranged comfortably for his master, the fires lighted, candles prepared, dressing-gown and slippers in their place, and aired, and everything in order that is required for his master's comforts.

6

Duties of Housemaids

Housemaids, in large establishments, have usually one or more assistants; in this case they are upper and under housemaids. Dividing the work between them, the upper housemaid will probably reserve for herself the task of dusting the ornaments and cleaning the furniture of the principal apartments, but it is her duty to see that every department is properly attended to. The number of assistants depends on the number in the family, as well as on the style in which the establishment is kept up.

In wealthy families it is not unusual for every grown-up daughter to have her waiting-maid, whose duty it is to keep her mistress's apartments in order, thus abridging the housemaid's duties. In others, perhaps, one waiting-maid attends on two or three, when the housemaid's assistance will be more requisite. In fact, every establishment has some customs peculiar to itself, on which we need not dwell; the general duties are the same in all, perfect cleanliness and order being the object.

"Cleanliness is next to godliness," saith the proverb, and "order" is in the next degree; the housemaid, then, may be said to be the handmaiden to two of the most prominent virtues. Her duties are very numerous, and many of the comforts of the family depend on their performance; but they are simple and easy to a person naturally clean and orderly, and desirous of giving satisfaction. In all families, whatever the habits of the master and mistress, servants will find it advantageous to rise early; their daily work will thus come easy to them.

If they rise late, there is a struggle to overtake it, which throws an air of haste and hurry over the whole establishment. Where the master's time is regulated by early business or professional engagements, this will, of course, regulate the hours of the servants; but even where that is not the case, servants will find great personal convenience in rising early and getting through their work in an orderly and methodical manner.

Cleaning

The housemaid who studies her own ease will certainly be at her work by six o'clock in the summer, and, probably, half-past six or seven in the winter months, having spent a reasonable time in her own chamber in dressing. Earlier than this would, probably, be an unnecessary waste of coals and candle in winter. The first duty of the housemaid in winter is to open the shutters of all the lower rooms in the house, and take up the hearth-rugs of those rooms which she is going to "do" before breakfast.

In some families, where there is only a cook and housemaid kept, and where the drawing-rooms are large, the cook has the care of the dining-room, and the housemaid that of the breakfast-room, library, and drawing-rooms. After the shutters are all opened, she sweeps the breakfast-room, sweeping the dust towards the fire-place, of course previously removing the fonder. She should then lay a cloth (generally made of coarse wrappering) over the carpet in front of the stove, and on this should place her housemaid's box, containing black-lead brushes, leathers, emery-paper, cloth, black lead, and all utensils necessary for cleaning a grate, with the cinder-pail on the other side. She now sweeps up the ashes, and deposits them in her cinder-pail, which is a japanned tin pail, with a wire-sifter inside, and a closely-fitting top. In this pail the cinders are sifted, and reserved for use in the kitchen or under the copper, the ashes only being thrown away.

The cinders disposed of, she proceeds to black-lead the grate, producing the black lead, the soft brush for laying it on, her blacking and polishing brushes, from the box which contains her tools. This housemaid's box should be kept well stocked. Having blackened, brushed, and polished every part, and made all clean and bright, she now proceeds to lay the fire. Sometimes it is very difficult to get a proper polish to black grates, particularly if they have been neglected, and allowed to rust at all. Brunswick black, which is an excellent varnish for grates, may be prepared in the following manner:--

Ingredients: 1 lb. of common asphaltum, 1/2 pint of linseed oil, 1 quart of oil of turpentine.

Mode: Melt the asphaltum, and add gradually to it the other two ingredients. Apply this with a small painter's brush, and leave it to become perfectly dry. The grate will need no other cleaning, but will merely require dusting every day, and occasionally brushing with a dry black-lead brush. This is, of course, when no fires are used. When they are required, the bars, cheeks, and back of the grate will need black-leading in the usual manner.

Fire-lighting, however simple, is an operation requiring some skill; a fire is readily made by laying a few cinders at the bottom in open order; over this a few pieces of paper, and over that again eight or ten pieces of dry wood; over the wood, a course of moderate-sized pieces of coal, taking care to leave hollow spaces between for air at the centre; and taking care to lay the whole well back in the grate, so that the smoke may go up the chimney, and not into the room. This done, fire the paper with a match from below, and, if properly laid, it will soon burn up; the stream of flame from the wood and paper soon communicating to the coals and cinders, provided there is plenty of air at the centre.

A new method of lighting a fire is sometimes practised with advantage, the fire lighting from the top and burning down, in place of being lighted and burning up from below. This is arranged by laying the coals at the bottom, mixed with a few good-sized cinders, and the wood at the top, with another layer of coals and some paper over it; the paper is lighted in the usual way, and soon burns down to a good fire, with some economy of fuel, as is said.

Bright grates require unceasing attention to keep them in perfect order. A day should never pass without the housemaid rubbing with a dry leather the polished parts of a grate, as also the fender and fire-irons. A careful and attentive housemaid should have no occasion ever to use emery-paper for any part but the bars, which, of course, become blackened by the fire. When bright grates are once neglected, small rust-spots begin to show themselves, which a plain leather will not remove; the following method of cleaning them must then be resorted to:

First, thoroughly clean with emery-paper; then take a large smooth pebble from the road, sufficiently large to hold comfortably in the hand, with which rub the steel backwards and forwards one way, until the desired polish is obtained. It may appear at first to scratch, but continue rubbing, and the result will be success. The following is also an excellent polish for bright stoves and steel articles:-

Ingredients: 1 tablespoonful of turpentine, 1 ditto of sweet oil, emery powder.

Mode: Mix the turpentine and sweet oil together, stirring in sufficient emery powder to make the mixture of the thickness of cream. Put it on the article with a piece of soft flannel, rub off quickly with another piece, then polish with a little dry emery powder and clean leather.

The several fires lighted, the housemaid proceeds with her dusting, and polishing the several pieces of furniture in the breakfast-parlour, leaving no corner unvisited. Before sweeping the carpet, it is a good practice to sprinkle it all over with tea-leaves, which not only lay all dust, but give a slightly fragrant smell to the room. It is now in order for the reception of the family; and where there is neither footman nor parlour-maid, she now proceeds to the dressing-room, and lights her mistress's fire, if she is in the habit of having one to dress by.

Her mistress is called, hot water placed in the dressing-room for her use, her clothes – as far as they are under the house-maid's charge – put before the fire to air, hanging a fire-guard on the bars where there is one, while she proceeds to prepare the breakfast.

In summer the housemaid's work is considerably abridged: she throws open the windows of the several rooms not occupied as bedrooms, that they may receive the fresh morning air before they are occupied; she prepares the breakfast-room by sweeping the carpet, rubbing tables and chairs, dusting mantel-shelf and picture-frames with a light brush, dusting the furniture, and beating and sweeping the rug; she cleans the grate when necessary, and replaces the white paper or arranges the shavings with which it is filled, leaving everything clean and tidy for breakfast.

It is not enough, however, in cleaning furniture, just to pass lightly over the surface; the rims and legs of tables, and the backs and legs of chairs and sofas, should be rubbed vigorously daily; if there is a book-case, every corner of every pane and ledge requires to be carefully wiped, so that not a speck of dust can be found in the room.

After the breakfast-room is finished, the housemaid should proceed to sweep down the stairs, commencing at the top, whilst the cook has the charge of the hall, door-step, and passages. After this she should go into the drawing-room, cover up every article of furniture that is likely to spoil, with large dusting-sheets, and put the chairs together, by turning them seat to seat, and, in fact, make as much room as possible, by placing all the loose furniture in the middle of the room, whilst she sweeps the corners and sides.

When this is accomplished, the furniture can then be put back in its place, and the middle of the room swept, sweeping the dirt, as before said, towards the fireplace. The same rules should be observed in cleaning the drawing-room grates as we have just stated, putting down the cloth, before commencing, to prevent the carpet from getting soiled. In the country, a room would not require sweeping thoroughly like this more than twice a week; but the housemaid should go over it every morning with a dust-pan and broom, taking up every crumb and piece she may see.

After the sweeping she should leave the room, shut the door, and proceed to lay the breakfast. Where there is neither footman nor parlour-maid kept, the duty of laying the breakfast-cloth rests on the housemaid. Before laying the cloth for breakfast, the heater of the tea-urn is to be placed in the hottest part of the kitchen fire; or, where the kettle is used, boiled on the kitchen fire, and then removed to the parlour, where it is kept hot.

Having washed herself free from the dust arising from the morning's work, the housemaid collects the breakfast-things on her tray, takes the breakfast-cloth from the napkin press, and carries them all on the tray into the parlour; arranges them on the table, placing a sufficiency of knives, forks, and salt-cellars for the family, and takes the tray back to the pantry; gets a supply of milk, cream, and bread; fills the butter-dish, taking care that the salt is plentiful, and soft and dry, and that hot plates and egg-cups are ready where warm meat or eggs are served; and that butter-knife and bread-knife are in their places.

And now she should give the signal for breakfast, holding herself ready to fill the urn with hot water, or hand the kettle, and take in the rolls, toast, and other eatables, with which the cook supplies her, when the breakfast-room bell rings; bearing in mind that she is never to enter the parlour with dirty hands or with a dirty apron, and that everything is to be handed on a tray; that she is to hand everything she may be required to supply, on the left hand of the person she is serving, and that all is done quietly and without bustle or hurry.

In some families, where there is a large number to attend on, the cook waits at breakfast whilst the housemaid is busy upstairs in the bedrooms, or sweeping, dusting, and putting the drawing-room in order. Breakfast served, the housemaid proceeds to the bed-chambers, throws up the sashes, if not already done, pulls up the blinds, throwing back curtains at the same time, and opens the beds, by removing the clothes, placing them over a horse, or, failing that, over the backs of chairs. She now proceeds to empty the slops.

In doing this, everything is emptied into the slop-pail, leaving a little scalding-hot water for a minute in such vessels as require it; adding a drop of turpentine to the water, when that is not sufficient to cleanse them. The basin is emptied, well rinsed with clean water, and carefully wiped; the ewers emptied and washed; finally, the water-jugs themselves emptied out and rinsed, and wiped dry. As soon as this is done, she should remove and empty the pails, taking care that they also are well washed, scalded, and wiped as soon as they are empty. Next follows bedmaking, at which the cook or kitchen-maid, where one is kept, usually assists; but, before beginning, velvet chairs, or other things injured by dust, should be removed to another room.

Arrangement of Rooms

In bedmaking, the fancy of its occupant should be consulted; some like beds sloping from the top towards the feet, swelling slightly in the middle; others, perfectly flat: a good housemaid will accommodate each bed to the taste of the sleeper, taking care to shake, beat, and turn it well in the process. Some persons prefer sleeping on the mattress; in which case a feather bed is usually beneath, resting on a second mattress, and a straw paillasse at the bottom.

In this case, the mattresses should change places daily; the feather bed placed on the mattress shaken, beaten, taken up and opened several times, so as thoroughly to separate the feathers: if too large to be thus handled, the maid should shake and beat one end first, and then the other, smoothing it afterwards equally all over into the required shape, and place the mattress gently over it. Any feathers which escape in this process a tidy servant will put back through the seam of the tick; she will also be careful to sew up any stitch that gives way the moment it is discovered.

The bedclothes are laid on, beginning with an under blanket and sheet, which are tucked under the mattress at the bottom. The bolster is then beaten and shaken, and put on, the top of the sheet rolled round it, and the sheet tucked in all round. The pillows and other bedclothes follow, and the counterpane over all, which should fall in graceful folds, and at equal distance from the ground all round. The curtains are drawn to the head and folded neatly across the bed, and the whole finished in a smooth and graceful manner.

Where spring-mattresses are used, care should be taken that the top one is turned every day. The housemaid should now take up in a dustpan any pieces that may be on the carpet; she should dust the room, shut the door, and proceed to another room. When all the bedrooms are finished, she should dust the stairs, and polish the handrail of the banisters, and see that all ledges, window-sills, &c., are quite free from dust. It will be necessary for the housemaid to divide her work, so that she may not have too much to do on certain days, and not sufficient to fill up her time on other days.

In the country, bedrooms should be swept and thoroughly cleaned once a week; and to be methodical and regular in her work, the housemaid should have certain days for doing certain rooms thoroughly. For instance, the drawing-room on Monday, two bedrooms on Tuesday, two on Wednesday, and so on, reserving a day for thoroughly cleaning the plate, bedroom candlesticks, &c. &c., which she will have to do where there is no parlour-maid or footman kept. By this means the work will be divided, and there will be no unnecessary bustling and hurrying, as is the case where the work is done any time, without rule or regulation.

Once a week, when a bedroom is to be thoroughly cleaned, the house-maid should commence by brushing the mattresses of the bed before it is made; she should then make it, shake the curtains, lay them smoothly on the bed, and pin or tuck up the bottom valance, so that she may be able to sweep under the bed. She should then unloop the window-curtains, shake them, and pin them high up out of the way. After clearing the dressing-table, and the room altogether of little articles of china, &c. &c., she should shake the toilet-covers, fold them up, and lay them on the bed, over which a large dusting-sheet should be thrown.

She should then sweep the room; first of all sprinkling the carpet with well-squeezed tea-leaves, or a little freshly-pulled grass, when this is obtainable. After the carpet is swept, and the grate cleaned, she should wash with soap and water, with a little soda in it, the washing-table apparatus, removing all marks or fur round the jugs, caused by the water. The water-bottles and tumblers must also have her attention, as well as the top of the washing-stand, which should be cleaned with soap and flannel if it be marble: if of polished mahogany, no soap must be used.

When these are all clean and arranged in their places, the housemaid should scrub the floor where it is not covered with carpet, under the beds, and round the wainscot. She should use as little soap and soda as possible, as too free a use of these articles is liable to give the boards a black appearance. In the country, cold soft water, a clean scrubbing-brush, and a willing arm, are all that are required to make bedroom floors look white. In winter it is not advisable to scrub rooms too often, as it is difficult to dry them thoroughly at that season of the year, and nothing is more dangerous than to allow persons to sleep in a damp room.

The housemaid should now dust the furniture, blinds, ornaments, etc.; polish the looking-glass; arrange the toilet-cover and muslin; remove the cover from the bed, and straighten and arrange the curtains and counterpane. A bedroom should be cleaned like this every week. There are times, however, when it is necessary to have the carpet up; this should be done once a year in the country, and twice a year in large cities. The best time for these arrangements is spring and autumn, when the bed-furniture requires changing to suit the seasons of the year.

After arranging the furniture, it should all be well rubbed and polished; and for this purpose the housemaid should provide herself with an old silk pocket-handkerchief, to finish the polishing. As modern furniture is now nearly always French-polished, it should often be rubbed with an old silk rubber, or a fine cloth or duster, to keep it free from smears. Three or four times a year any of the following polishes may be applied with very great success, as any of them make French-polished furniture look very well. One precaution must be taken,-- not to put too much of the polish on at one time, and to rub, not smear it over the articles.

Furniture Polish:

Ingredients: 1/4 pint of linseed-oil, 1/4 pint of vinegar, 1 oz. of spirits of salts, 1/2 oz. of muriatic antimony.

Mode: Mix all well together, and shake before using.

Ingredients: Equal proportions of linseed-oil, turpentine, vinegar, and spirits of wine.

Mode: When used, shake the mixture well, and rub on the furniture with a piece of linen rag, and polish with a clean duster. Vinegar and oil, rubbed in with flannel, and the furniture rubbed with a clean duster, produce a very good polish.

Furniture Paste:

Ingredients: 3 oz. of common beeswax, 1 oz. of white wax, 1 oz. of curd soap, 1 pint of turpentine, 1 pint of boiled water.

Mode: Mix the ingredients together, adding the water when cold; shake the mixture frequently in the bottle, and do not use it for 48 hours after it is made. It should be applied with a piece of flannel, the furniture polished with a duster, and then with an old silk rubber.

The chambers are finished, the chamber candlesticks brought down and cleaned, the parlour lamps trimmed;– and here the housemaid's utmost care is required. In cleaning candlesticks, as in every other cleaning, she should have cloths and brushes kept for that purpose alone; the knife used to scrape them should be applied to no other purpose; the tallow-grease should be thrown into a box kept for the purpose; the same with everything connected with the lamp-trimming; the best mode of doing which she will do well to learn from the tradesman who supplies the oil; always bearing in mind, however, that without perfect cleanliness, which involves occasional scalding, no lamp can be kept in order.

The drawing and dining-room, inasmuch as everything there is more costly and valuable, require even more care. When the carpets are of the kind known as velvet-pile, they require to be swept firmly by a hard whisk brush, made of cocoanut fibre. The furniture must be carefully gone over in every corner with a soft cloth, that it may be left perfectly free from dust; or where that is beyond reach, with a brush made of long feathers, or a goose's wing. The sofas are swept in the same manner, slightly beaten, the cushions shaken and smoothed, the picture-frames swept, and everything arranged in its proper place.

This, of course, applies to dining as well as drawing-room and morning-room. And now the housemaid may dress herself for the day, and prepare for the family dinner, at which she must attend. We need not repeat the long instructions already given for laying the dinner-table. At the family dinner, even where no footman waits, the routine will be the same. In most families the cloth is laid with the slips on each side, with napkins, knives, forks, spoons, and wine and finger glasses on all occasions.

She should ascertain that her plate is in order, glasses free from smears, water-bottles and decanters the same, and everything ready on her tray, that she may be able to lay her cloth properly. Few things add more to the neat and comfortable appearance of a dinner-table than well-polished plate; indeed, the state of the plate is a certain indication of a well-managed or ill-managed household. Nothing is easier than to keep plate in good order, and yet many servants, from stupidity and ignorance, make it the greatest trouble of all things under their care.

It should be remembered, that it is utterly impossible to make greasy silver take a polish; and that as spoons and forks in daily use are continually in contact with grease, they must require good washing in soap-and-water to remove it. Silver should be washed with a soapy flannel in one water, rinsed in another, and then wiped dry with a dry cloth. The plate so washed may be polished with the plate-rags, as in the following directions:-- Once a week all the plate should receive a thorough cleaning with the hartshorn powder, as directed in the first recipe for cleaning plate; and where the housemaid can find time, rubbed every day with the plate-rags.

Hartshorn is one of the best possible ingredients for plate-powder in daily use. It leaves on the silver a deep, dark polish, and at the same time does less injury than anything else. It has also the advantage of being very cheap; almost all the ordinary powders sold in boxes containing more or less of quicksilver, in some form or another; and this in process of time is sure to make the plate brittle. If any one wishes to be convinced of the effect of quicksilver on plate, he has only to rub a little of it on one place for some time, – on the handle of a silver teaspoon for instance, and he will find it break in that spot with very little pressure.

Dishwashing

Wash the plate well to remove all grease, in a strong lather of common yellow soap and boiling water, and wipe it quite dry; then mix as much hartshorn powder as will be required, into a thick paste, with cold water or spirits of wine; smear this lightly over the plate with a piece of soft rag, and leave it for some little time to dry. When perfectly dry, brush it off quite clean with a soft plate-brush, and polish the plate with a dry leather. If the plate be very dirty, or much tarnished, spirits of wine will be found to answer better than the water for mixing the paste.

Plate-rags for daily use: Boil soft rags in a mixture of new milk and hartshorn powder, in the proportion of 1 oz. of powder to a pint of milk; boil them for 5 minutes; wring them as soon as they are taken out, for a moment, in cold water, and dry them before the fire. With these rags rub the plate briskly as soon as it has been well washed and dried after daily use. A most beautiful deep polish will be produced, and the plate will require nothing more than merely to be dusted with a leather or a dry soft cloth, before it is again put on the table.

Food Serving

For waiting at table, the housemaid should be neatly and cleanly dressed, and, if possible, her dress made with closed sleeves, the large open ones dipping and falling into everything on the table, and being very much in the way. She should not wear creaking boots, and should move about the room as noiselessly as possible, anticipating people's wants by handing them things without being asked for them, and altogether be as quiet as possible. It will be needless here to repeat what we have already said respecting waiting at table, in the duties of the butler and footman: rules that are good to be observed by them, are equally good for the parlour-maid or housemaid.

The housemaid having announced that dinner is on the table, will hand the soup, fish, meat, or side-dishes to the different members of the family; but in families who do not spend much of the day together, they will probably prefer being alone at dinner and breakfast; the housemaid will be required, after all are helped, if her master does not wish her to stay in the room, to go on with her work of cleaning up in the pantry, and answer the bell when rung. In this case she will place a pile of plates on the table or a dumbwaiter, within reach of her master and mistress, and leave the room.

Dinner over, the housemaid removes the plates and dishes on the tray, places the dirty knives and forks in the basket prepared for them, folds up the napkins in the ring which indicates by which member of the family it has been used, brushes off the crumbs on the hand-tray kept for the purpose, folds up the table-cloth in the folds already made, and places it in the linen-press to be smoothed out.

After every meal the table should be rubbed, all marks from hot plates removed, and the table-cover thrown over, and the room restored to its usual order. If the family retire to the drawing-room, or any other room, it is a good practice to throw up the sash to admit fresh air and ventilate the room.

The housemaid's evening service consists in washing up the dinner-things, the plate, plated articles, and glasses, restoring everything to its place; cleaning up her pantry, and putting away everything for use when next required; lastly, preparing for tea, as the time approaches, by setting the things out on the tray, getting the urn or kettle ready, with cream and other things usually partaken of at that meal.

In summer-time the windows of all the bedrooms, which have been closed during the heat of the day, should be thrown open for an hour or so after sunset, in order to air them. Before dark they should be closed, the bedclothes turned down, and the night-clothes laid in order for use when required. During winter, where fires are required in the dressing-rooms, they should be lighted an hour before the usual time of retiring, placing a fire-guard before each fire.

At the same time, the night-things on the horse should be placed before it to be aired, with a tin can of hot water, if the mistress is in the habit of washing before going to bed. We may add, that there is no greater preservative of beauty than washing the face every night in hot water. The housemaid will probably be required to assist her mistress to undress and put her dress in order for the morrow; in which case her duties are very much those of the lady's-maid.

And now the fire is made up for the night, the fireguard replaced, and everything in the room in order for the night, the housemaid taking care to leave the night-candle and matches together in a convenient place, should they be required. It is usual in summer to remove all highly fragrant flowers from sleeping-rooms, the impression being that their scent is injurious in a close chamber.

On leisure days, the housemaid should be able to do some needlework for her mistress,-- such as turning and mending sheets and darning the house linen, or assist her in anything she may think fit to give her to do. For this reason it is almost essential that a housemaid, in a small family, should be an expert needlewoman; as, if she be a good manager and an active girl, she will have time on her hands to get through plenty of work.

Periodical Cleanings

Besides the daily routine which we have described, there are portions of every house which can only be thoroughly cleaned occasionally; at which time the whole house usually undergoes a more thorough cleaning than is permitted in the general way. On these occasions it is usual to begin at the top of the house and clean downwards;

moving everything out of the room; washing the wainscoting or paint with soft soap and water; pulling down the beds and thoroughly cleansing all the joints; "scrubbing" the floor; beating feather beds, mattress, and paillasse, and thoroughly purifying every article of furniture before it is put back in its place.

This general cleaning usually takes place in the spring or early summer, when the warm curtains of winter are replaced by the light and cheerful muslin curtains. Carpets are at the same time taken up and beaten, except where the mistress of the house has been worried into an experiment by the often-reiterated question, "Why beat your carpets?" In this case she will probably have made up her mind to try the cleaning process, and arranged with the company to send for them on the morning when cleaning commenced. It is hardly necessary to repeat, that on this occasion every article is to be gone over, the French-polished furniture well rubbed and polished.

The same thorough system of cleaning should be done throughout the house; the walls cleaned where painted, and swept down with a soft broom or feather brush where papered; the window and bed curtains, which have been replaced with muslin ones, carefully brushed, or, if they require it, cleaned; lamps not likely to be required, washed out with hot water, dried, and cleaned. The several grates are now to be furnished with their summer ornaments; and we know none prettier than the following, which the housemaid may provide at a small expense to her mistress: –

Purchase two yards and a half of crinoline muslin, and tear it into small strips, the selvage way of the material, about an inch wide; strip this thread by thread on each side, leaving the four centre threads; this gives about six-and-thirty pieces, fringed on each side, which are tied together at one end, and fastened to the trap of the register, while the threads, unravelled, are spread gracefully about the grate, the lower part of which is filled with paper shavings. This makes a very elegant and very cheap ornament, which is much stronger, besides, than those usually purchased.

As winter approaches, this house-cleaning will have to be repeated, and the warm bed and window curtains replaced. The process of scouring and cleaning is again necessary, and must be gone through, beginning at the top, and going through the house, down to the kitchens. Independently of these daily and periodical cleanings, other occupations will present themselves from time to time, which the housemaid will have to perform. When spots show on polished furniture, they can generally be restored by soap-and-water and a sponge, the polish being brought out by using a little polish, and then well rubbing it.

Again, drawers which draw out stiffly may be made to move more easily if the spot where they press is rubbed over with a little soap. Chips broken off any of the furniture should be collected and replaced, by means of a little glue applied to it. Liquid glue, which is sold prepared in bottles, is very useful to have in the house, as it requires no melting; and anything broken can be so quickly repaired.

Breaking glass and china is about the most disagreeable thing that can happen in a family, and it is, probably, a greater annoyance to a right-minded servant than to the mistress. A neat-handed housemaid may sometimes repair these breakages, where they are not broken in very conspicuous places, by joining the pieces very neatly together with a cement made as follows:

Dissolve an ounce of gum mastic in a quantity of highly-rectified spirits of wine; then soften an ounce of isinglass in warm water, and, finally, dissolve it in rum or brandy, till it forms a thick jelly. Mix the isinglass and gum mastic together, adding a quarter of an ounce of finely-powdered gum ammoniac; put the whole into an earthen pipkin, and in a warm place, till they are thoroughly incorporated together; pour it into a small phial, and cork it down for use.

In using it, dissolve a small piece of the cement in a silver teaspoon over a lighted candle. The broken pieces of glass or china being warmed, and touched with the now liquid cement, join the parts neatly together, and hold in their places till the cement has set; then wipe away the cement adhering to the edge of the joint, and leave it for twelve hours without touching it: the joint will be as strong as the china itself, and if neatly done, it will show no joining. It is essential that neither of the pieces be wetted either with hot or cold water.

Useful Recipes for Housemaids

To clean Marble: Mix with 1/4 pint of soap lees, 1/2 gill of turpentine, sufficient pipe-clay and bullock's gall to make the whole into rather a thick paste. Apply it to the marble with a soft brush, and after a day or two, when quite dry, rub it off with a soft rag. Apply this a second or third time till the marble is quite clean.

Take two parts of soda, one of pumice-stone, and one of finely-powdered chalk. Sift these through a fine sieve, and mix them into a paste with water. Rub this well all over the marble, and the stains will be removed; then wash it with soap-and-water, and a beautiful bright polish will be produced.

To clean Floorcloth: After having washed the floorcloth in the usual manner with a damp flannel, wet it all over with milk and rub it well with a dry cloth, when a most beautiful polish will be brought out. Some persons use for rubbing a well-waxed flannel; but this in general produces an unpleasant slipperiness, which is not the case with the milk.

To clean Decanters: Roll up in small pieces some soft brown or blotting paper; wet them, and soap them well. Put them into the decanters about one quarter full of warm water; shake them well for a few minutes, then rinse with clear cold water; wipe the outsides with a nice dry cloth, put the decanters to drain, and when dry they will be almost as bright as new ones.

To brighten Gilt Frames: Take sufficient flour of sulphur to give a golden tinge to about 1-1/2 pint of water, and in this boil 4 or 5 bruised onions, or garlic, which will answer the same purpose. Strain off the liquid, and with it, when cold, wash, with a soft brush, any gilding which requires restoring, and when dry it will come out as bright as new work.

Fire-irons from Rust

Make a strong paste of fresh lime and water, and with a fine brush smear it as thickly as possible over all the polished surface requiring preservation. By this simple means, all the grates and fire-irons in an empty house may be kept for months free from harm, without further care or attention.

German Furniture-Gloss

Ingredients: 1/2 lb. yellow wax, 1 oz. black rosin, 2 oz. of oil of turpentine.

Mode: Cut the wax into small pieces, and melt it in a pipkin, with the rosin pounded very fine. Stir in gradually, while these two ingredients are quite warm, the oil of turpentine. Keep this composition well covered for use in a tin or earthen pot. A little of this gloss should be spread on a piece of coarse woollen cloth, and the furniture well rubbed with it; afterwards it should be polished with a fine cloth.

The general servant, or maid-of-all-work, is perhaps the only one of her class deserving of commiseration: her life is a solitary one, and in, some places, her work is never done. She is also subject to rougher treatment than either the house or kitchen-maid, especially in her earlier career: she starts in life, probably a girl of thirteen, with some small tradesman's wife as her mistress, just a step above her in the social scale; and although the class contains among them many excellent, kind-hearted women, it also contains some very rough specimens of the feminine gender, and to some of these it occasionally falls to give our maid-of-all-work her first lessons in her multifarious occupations: the mistress's commands are the measure of the maid-of-all-work's duties.

By the time she has become a tolerable servant, she is probably engaged in some respectable tradesman's house, where she has to rise with the lark, for she has to do in her own person all the work which in larger establishments is performed by cook, kitchen-maid, and housemaid, and occasionally the part of a footman's duty, which consists in carrying messages.

The general servant's duties commence by opening the shutters of all the lower apartments in the house; she should then brush up her kitchen-range, light the fire, clear away the ashes, clean the hearth, and polish with a leather the bright parts of the range, doing all as rapidly and as vigorously as possible, that no more time be wasted than is necessary. After putting on the kettle, she should then proceed to the dining-room or parlour to get it in order for breakfast.

She should first roll up the rug, take up the fender, shake and fold up the table-cloth, then sweep the room, carrying the dirt towards the fireplace; a coarse cloth should then be laid down over the carpet, and she should proceed to clean the grate, having all her utensils close to her. When the grate is finished, the ashes cleared away, the hearth cleaned, and the fender put back in its place, she must dust the furniture, not omitting the legs of the tables and chairs; and if there are any ornaments or things on the sideboard, she must not dust round them, but lift them up on to another place, dust well where they have been standing, and then replace the things.

Nothing annoys a particular mistress so much as to find, when she comes down stairs, different articles of furniture looking as if they had never been dusted. If the servant is at all methodical, and gets into a habit of doing a room in a certain way, she will scarcely ever leave her duties neglected. After the rug is put down, the table-cloth arranged, and everything in order, she should lay the cloth for breakfast, and then shut the dining-room door.

The hall must now be swept, the mats shaken, the door-step cleaned, and any brass knockers or handles polished up with the leather. If the family breakfast very early, the tidying of the hall must then be deferred till after that meal. After cleaning the boots that are absolutely required, the servant should now wash her hands and face, put on a clean white apron, and be ready for her mistress when she comes down stairs.

In families where there is much work to do before breakfast, the master of the house frequently has two pairs of boots in wear, so that they may be properly cleaned when the servant has more time to do them, in the daytime. This arrangement is, perhaps, scarcely necessary in the summer-time, when there are no grates to clean every morning; but in the dark days of winter it is only kind and thoughtful to lighten a servant-of-all-work's duties as much as possible.

She will now carry the urn into the dining-room, where her mistress will make the tea or coffee, and sometimes will boil the eggs, to insure them being done to her liking. In the mean time the servant cooks, if required, the bacon, kidneys, fish, &c – if cold meat is to be served, she must always send it to table on a clean dish, and nicely garnished with tufts of parsley, if this is obtainable.

After she has had her own breakfast, and whilst the family are finishing theirs, she should go upstairs into the bedrooms, open all the windows, strip the clothes off the beds, and leave them to air whilst she is clearing away the breakfast things. She should then take up the crumbs in a dustpan from under the table, put the chairs in their places, and sweep up the hearth.

The breakfast things washed up, the kitchen should be tidied, so that it may be neat when her mistress comes in to give the orders for the day: after receiving these orders, the servant should go upstairs again, with a jug of boiling water, the slop-pail, and two cloths. After emptying the slops, and scalding the vessels with the boiling water, and wiping them thoroughly dry, she should wipe the top of the wash-table and arrange it all in order. She then proceeds to make the beds, in which occupation she is generally assisted by the mistress, or, if she have any daughters, by one of them.

Before commencing to make the bed, the servant should put on a large bed-apron, kept for this purpose only, which should be made very wide, to button round the waist and meet behind, while it should be made as long as the dress. By adopting this plan, the blacks and dirt on servants' dresses will not rub off on to the bed-clothes, mattresses, and bed furniture. When the beds are made, the rooms should be dusted, the stairs lightly swept down, hall furniture, closets, &c., dusted.

The lady of the house, where there is but one servant kept, frequently takes charge of the drawing-room herself, that is to say, dusting it; the servant sweeping, cleaning windows, looking-glasses, grates, and rough work of that sort. If there are many ornaments and knick-knacks about the room, it is certainly better for the mistress to dust these herself, as a maid-of-all-work's hands are not always in a condition to handle delicate ornaments.

Now she has gone the rounds of the house and seen that all is in order, the servant goes to her kitchen to see about the cooking of the dinner, in which very often her mistress will assist her. She should put on a coarse apron with a bib to do her dirty work in, which may be easily replaced by a white one if required.

Half an hour before dinner is ready, she should lay the cloth, that everything may be in readiness when she is dishing up the dinner, and take all into the dining-room that is likely to be required, in the way of knives, forks, spoons, bread, salt, water, &c. &c. By exercising a little forethought, much confusion and trouble may be saved both to mistress and servant, by getting everything ready for the dinner in good time.

After taking in the dinner, when every one is seated, she removes the covers, hands the plates round, and pours out the beer; and should be careful to hand everything on the left side of the person she is waiting on. We need scarcely say that a maid-of-all-work cannot stay in the dining-room during the whole of dinner-time, as she must dish up her pudding, or whatever is served after the first course. When she sees every one helped, she should leave the room to make her preparations for the next course; and anything that is required, such as bread, &c., people may assist themselves to in the absence of the servant.

When the dinner things are cleared away, the servant should sweep up the crumbs in the dining-room, sweep the hearth, and lightly dust the furniture, then sit down to her own dinner. After this, she washes up and puts away the dinner things, sweeps the kitchen, dusts and tidies it, and puts on the kettle for tea. She should now, before dressing herself for the afternoon, clean her knives, boots, and shoes, and do any other dirty work in the scullery that may be necessary.

Knife-cleaning machines are rapidly taking the place, in most households, of the old knife-board. The saving of labour by the knife-cleaner is very great, and its performance of the work is very satisfactory. Small and large machines are manufactured, some cleaning only four knives, whilst others clean as many as twelve at once. Nothing can be more simple than the process of machine knife-cleaning; and although, in a very limited household, the substitution of the machine for the board may not be necessary, yet we should advise all housekeepers, to whom the outlay is not a difficulty, to avail themselves of the services of a machine.

When the servant is dressed, she takes in the tea, and after tea turns down the beds, sees that the water-jugs and bottles are full, closes the windows, and draws down the blinds. If the weather is very warm, these are usually left open until the last thing at night, to cool the rooms. The routine of a general servant's duties depends upon the kind of situation she occupies; but a systematic maid-of-all-work should so contrive to divide her work, that every day in the week may have its proper share.

By this means she is able to keep the house clean with less fatigue to herself than if she left all the cleaning to do at the end of the week. Supposing there are five bedrooms in the house, two sitting-rooms, kitchen, scullery, and the usual domestic offices: – on Monday she should thoroughly clean the drawing-room; on Tuesday, two of the bedrooms; on Wednesday, two more; on Thursday, the other bedroom and stairs; on Friday morning she should sweep the dining-room very thoroughly, clean the hall, and in the afternoon her kitchen tins and bright utensils.

By arranging her work in this manner, no undue proportion will fall to Saturday's share, and she will then have this day for cleaning plate, cleaning her kitchen, and arranging everything in nice order. The regular work must, of course, be performed in the usual manner, as we have endeavoured to describe. Before retiring to bed, she will do well to clean up glasses, plates, &c. which have been used for the evening meal, and prepare for her morning's work by placing her wood near the fire, on the hob, to dry, taking care there is no danger of it igniting, before she leaves the kitchen for the night. Before retiring, she will have to lock and bolt the doors, unless the master undertakes this office himself.

If the washing, or even a portion of it, is done at home, it will be impossible for the maid-of-all-work to do her household duties thoroughly, during the time it is about, unless she have some assistance. Usually, if all the washing is done at home, the mistress hires some one to assist at the wash-tub, and sees to little matters herself, in the way of dusting, clearing away breakfast things, folding, starching, and ironing the fine things. With a little management much can be accomplished, provided the mistress be industrious, energetic, and willing to lend a helping hand.

Let washing-week be not the excuse for having everything in a muddle; and although "things" cannot be cleaned so thoroughly, and so much time spent upon them, as ordinarily, yet the house may be kept tidy and clear from litter without a great deal of exertion either on the part of the mistress or servant.

With respect to the great wash – "Amongst all the occasions in which it is most difficult and glorious to keep muddle out of a family, 'the great wash' stands pre-eminent; and as very little money is now saved by having everything done at home, many ladies, with the option of taking another servant or putting out the chief part of the washing, have thankfully adopted the latter course." She goes on to say –

"When a gentleman who dines at home can't bear washing in the house, but gladly pays for its being done elsewhere, the lady should gratefully submit to his wishes, and put out anything in her whole establishment rather than put out a good and generous husband." A bustling and active girl will always find time to do a little needlework for herself, if she lives with consistent and reasonable people. In the summer evenings she should manage to sit down for two or three hours, and for a short time in the afternoon in leisure days.

A general servant's duties are so multifarious, that unless she be quick and active, she will not be able to accomplish this. To discharge these various duties properly is a difficult task, and sometimes a thankless office; but it must be remembered that a good maid-of-all-work will make a good servant in any capacity, and may be safely taken not only without fear of failure, but with every probability of giving satisfaction to her employer.

Duties of Dairy-maid

The duties of the dairy-maid differ considerably in different districts. In Scotland, Wales, and some of the northern counties, women milk the cows. On some of the large dairy farms in other parts of England, she takes her share in the milking, but in private families the milking is generally performed by the cowkeeper, and the dairy-maid only receives the milkpails from him morning and night, and empties and cleans them preparatory to the next milking; her duty being to supply the family with milk, cream, and butter, and other luxuries depending on the "milky mothers" of the herd.

The object with which gentlemen keep cows is to procure milk unadulterated, and sweet butter, for themselves and families: in order to obtain this, however, great cleanliness is required, and as visitors, as well as the mistress of the house, sometimes visit the dairy, some efforts are usually made to render it ornamental and picturesque. The locality is usually fixed near to the house; it should neither be exposed to the fierce heat of the summer's sun nor to the equally unfavourable frosts of winter – it must be both sheltered and shaded.

If it is a building apart from the house and other offices, the walls should be tolerably thick, and if hollow, the temperature will be more equable. The walls inside are usually covered with Dutch glazed tiles; the flooring also of glazed tiles set in asphalte, to resist water; and the ceiling, lath and plaster, or closely-jointed woodwork, painted. Its architecture will be a matter of fancy: it should have a northern aspect, and a thatched roof is considered most suitable, from the shade and shelter it affords; and it should contain at least two apartments, besides a cool place for storing away butter.

One of the apartments, in which the milk is placed to deposit cream, or to ripen for churning, is usually surrounded by shelves of marble or slate, on which the milk-dishes rest; but it will be found a better plan to have a large square or round table of stone in the centre, with a water-tight ledge all round it, in which water may remain in hot weather, or, if some attempt at the picturesque is desired, a small fountain might occupy the centre, which would keep the apartment cool and fresh.

Round this table the milk-dishes should be ranged; one shelf, or dresser, of slate or marble, being kept for the various occupations of the dairy-maid: it will be found a better plan than putting them on shelves and corners against the wall. There should be a funnel or ventilator in the ceiling, communicating with the open air, made to open and shut as required. Double windows are recommended, but of the lattice kind, so that they may open, and with wire-gauze blinds fitted into the opening, and calico blinds, which may be wetted when additional coolness is required.

The other apartment will be used for churning, washing, and scrubbing – in fact, the scullery of the dairy, with a boiler for hot water, and a sink with cold water laid on, which should be plentiful and good. In some dairies a third apartment, or, at least, a cool airy pantry, is required for storing away butter, with shelves of marble or slate, to hold the cream-jars while it is ripening; and where cheeses are made, a fourth becomes necessary.

The dairy utensils are not numerous,– churns, milk-pails for each cow, hair-sieves, slices of tin, milk-pans, marble dishes for cream for family use, scales and weights, a portable rack for drying the utensils, wooden bowls, butter-moulds and butter-patters, and wooden tubs for washing the utensils, comprising pretty nearly everything. Pails are made of maple-wood or elm, and hooped, or of tin, more or less ornamented. One is required for each cow.

The Hair-Sieve is made of closely-twisted horse-hair, with a rim, through which the milk is strained to remove any hairs which may have dropped from the cow in milking. Milk-Dishes are shallow basins of glass, of glazed earthenware, or tin, about 16 inches in diameter at top, and 12 at the bottom, and 5 or 6 inches deep, holding about 8 to 10 quarts each when full.

Churns are of all sorts and sizes, from that which churns 70 or 80 gallons by means of a strap from the engine, to the square box in which a pound of butter is made. The churn used for families is a square box, 18 inches by 12 or 13, and 17 deep, bevelled below to the plane of the dashers, with a loose lid or cover.

The dasher consists of an axis of wood, to which the four beaters or fanners are attached; these fans are simply four pieces of elm strongly dovetailed together, forming an oblong square, with a space left open, two of the openings being left broader than the others; attached to an axle, they form an axis with four projecting blades; the axle fits into supports at the centre of the box; a handle is fitted to it, and the act of churning is done by turning the handle. Such is the temple in which the dairy-maid presides: it should be removed both from stable and cowhouse, and larder; no animal smells should come near it, and the drainage should be perfect.

The dairy-maid receives the milk from the cowkeeper, each pail being strained through the hair-sieve into one of the milk-basins. This is left in the basins from twenty-four to thirty-six hours in the summer, according to the weather; after which it is skimmed off by means of the slicer, and poured into glazed earthenware jars to "turn" for churning.

Some persons prefer making up a separate churning for the milk of each cow; in which there is some advantage. In this case the basins of each cow, for two days, would either be kept together or labelled. As soon as emptied, the pails should be scalded and every particle of milk washed out, and placed away in a dry place till next required; and all milk spilt on the floor, or on the table or dresser, cleaned up with a cloth and hot water.

Where very great attention is paid to the dairy, the milk-coolers are used larger in winter, when it is desirable to retard the cooling down and increase the creamy deposit, and smaller in summer, to hasten it; the temperature required being from 55° to 50°. In summer it is sometimes expedient, in very sultry weather, to keep the dairy fresh and cool by suspending cloths dipped in chloride of lime across the room.

In some dairies it is usual to churn twice, and in others three times a week: the former produces the best butter, the other the greatest quantity. With three cows, the produce should be 27 to 30 quarts a day. The dairy-maid should churn every day when very hot, if they are in full milk, and every second day in more temperate weather; besides supplying the milk and cream required for a large establishment.

The churning should always be done in the morning: the dairy-maid will find it advantageous in being at work on churning mornings by five o'clock. The operation occupies from 20 minutes to half an hour in summer, and considerably longer in winter. A steady uniform motion is necessary to produce sweet butter; neither too quick nor too slow. Rapid motion causes the cream to heave and swell, from too much air being forced into it: the result is a tedious churning, and soft, bad-coloured butter.

In spring and summer, when the cow has her natural food, no artificial colour is required; but in winter, under stall-feeding, the colour is white and tallowy, and some persons prefer a higher colour. This is communicated by mixing a little finely-powdered arnotto with the cream before putting it into the churn; a still more, natural and delicate colour is communicated by scraping a red carrot into a clean piece of linen cloth, dipping it into water, and squeezing it into the cream.

As soon as the butter comes, the milk is poured off, and the butter put into a shallow wooden tub or bowl, full of pure spring water, in which it is washed and kneaded, pouring off the water, and renewing it until it comes away perfectly free from milk. Imperfect washing is the frequent cause of bad butter, and in nothing is the skill of the dairy-maid tested more than in this process;

moreover, it is one in which cleanliness of habits and person are most necessary.

In this operation we want the aid of Phyllis's neat, soft, and perfectly clean hand; for no mechanical operation can so well squeeze out the sour particles of milk or curd. The operations of churning and butter-making over, the butter-milk is disposed of: usually, in England, it goes to the pigs; but it is a, very wholesome beverage when fresh, and some persons like it; the disposal, therefore, will rest with the mistress: the dairy-maid's duty is to get rid of it. She must then scald with boiling water and scrub out every utensil she has used; brush out the churn, clean out the cream-jars, which will probably require the use of a little common soda to purify; wipe all dry, and place them in a position where the sun can reach them for a short time, to sweeten them.

In Devonshire, celebrated for its dairy system, the milk is always scalded. The milk-pans, which are of tin, and contain from 10 to 12 quarts, after standing 10 or 12 hours, are placed on a hot plate of iron, over a stove, until the cream has formed on the surface, which is indicated by the air-bubbles rising through the milk, and producing blisters on the surface-coating of cream. This indicates its approach to the boiling point: and the vessel is now removed to cool. When sufficiently, that is, quite cool, the cream is skimmed off with the slice: it is now the clouted cream for which Devonshire is so famous.

It is now placed in the churn, and churned until the butter comes, which it generally does in a much shorter time than by the other process. The butter so made contains more caseine than butter made in the usual way, but does not keep so long. It is a question frequently discussed, how far it is economical for families to keep cows and make their own butter. It is calculated that a good cow costs from May 1 to October 1, when well but economically kept, £5. 16s. 6d; and from October 1 to April

30, £10. 2s. 6d. During that time she should produce 227 lbs. of butter, besides the skimmed milk. Of course, if new milk and cream are required, that will diminish the quantity of butter.

Besides churning and keeping her dairy in order, the dairy-maid has charge of the whole produce, handing it over to the cook, butler, or housemaid as required; and she will do well to keep an exact account both of what she receives and how and when she disposes of it.

LAUNDRY-MAID

The laundry-maid is charged with the duty of washing and getting-up the family linen,– a situation of great importance where the washing is all done at home; but in large towns, where there is little convenience for bleaching and drying, it is chiefly done by professional laundresses and companies, who apply mechanical and chemical processes to the purpose. These processes, however, are supposed to injure the fabric of the linen; and in many families the fine linen, cottons, and muslins, are washed and got-up at home, even where the bulk of the washing is given out.

In country and suburban houses, where greater conveniences exist, washing at home is more common,-- in country places universal. The laundry establishment consists of a washing-house, an ironing and drying-room, and sometimes a drying-closet heated by furnaces. The washing-house will probably be attached to the kitchen; but it is better that it should be completely detached from it, and of one story, with a funnel or shaft to carry off the steam. It will be of a size proportioned to the extent of the washing to be done.

A range of tubs, either round or oblong, opposite to, and sloping towards, the light, narrower at the bottom than the top, for convenience in stooping over, and fixed at a height suited to the convenience of the women using them; each tub having a tap for hot and cold water, and another in the bottom, communicating with the drains, for drawing off foul water. A boiler and furnace, proportioned in size to the wants of the family, should also be fixed. The flooring should be York stone, laid on brick piers, with good drainage, or asphalte, sloping gently towards a gutter connected with the drain. Adjoining the bleaching-house, a second room, about the same size, is required for ironing, drying, and mangling.

The contents of this room should comprise an ironing-board, opposite to the light; a strong white deal table, about twelve or fourteen feet long, and about three and a half feet broad, with drawers for ironing-blankets; a mangle in one corner, and clothes-horses for drying and airing; cupboards for holding the various irons, starch, and other articles used in ironing; a hot-plate built in the chimney, with furnace beneath it for heating the irons; sometimes arranged with a flue for carrying the hot air round the room for drying.

Where this is the case, however, there should be a funnel in the ceiling for ventilation and carrying off steam; but a better arrangement is to have a hot-air closet adjoining, heated by hot-air pipes, and lined with iron, with proper arrangements for carrying off steam, and clothes-horses on castors running in grooves, to run into it for drying purposes. This leaves the laundry free from unwholesome vapour.

The laundry-maid should commence her labours on Monday morning by a careful examination of the articles committed to her care, and enter them in the washing-book; separating the white linen and collars, sheets and body-linen, into one heap, fine muslins into another, coloured cotton and linen fabrics into a third, woollens into a fourth, and the coarser kitchen and other greasy cloths into a fifth. Every article should be examined for ink- or grease-spots, or for fruit- or wine-stains.

Ink-spots are removed by dipping the part into hot water, and then spreading it smoothly on the hand or on the back of a spoon, pouring a few drops of oxalic acid or salts of sorel over the ink-spot, rubbing and rinsing it in cold water till removed; grease-spots, by rubbing over with yellow soap, and rinsing in hot water; fruit- and wine-spots, by dipping in a solution of sal ammonia or spirits of wine, and rinsing.

Every article having been examined and assorted, the sheets and fine linen should be placed in one of the tubs and just covered with lukewarm water, in which a little soda has been dissolved and mixed, and left there to soak till the morning. The greasy cloths and dirtier things should be laid to soak in another tub, in a liquor composed of 1/2 lb. of unslaked lime to every 6 quarts of water which has been boiled for two hours, then left to settle, and strained off when clear.

Each article should be rinsed in this liquor to wet it thoroughly, and left to soak till the morning, just covered by it when the things are pressed together. Coppers and boilers should now be filled, and the fires laid ready to light. Early on the following morning the fires should be lighted, and as soon as hot water can be procured, washing commenced; the sheets and body-linen being wanted to whiten in the morning, should be taken first; each article being removed in succession from the lye in which it has been soaking, rinsed, rubbed, and wrung, and laid aside until the tub is empty, when the foul water is drawn off.

The tub should be again filled with luke-warm water, about 80°, in which the articles should again be plunged, and each gone over carefully with soap, and rubbed. Novices in the art sometimes rub the linen against the skin; more experienced washerwomen rub one linen surface against the other, which saves their hands, and enables them to continue their labour much longer, besides economizing time, two parts being thus cleaned at once.

After this first washing, the linen should be put into a second water as hot as the hand can bear, and again rubbed over in every part, examining every part for spots not yet moved, which require to be again soaped over and rubbed till thoroughly clean; then rinsed and wrung, the larger and stronger articles by two of the women; the smaller and more delicate articles requiring gentler treatment.

In order to remove every particle of soap, and produce a good colour, they should now be placed, and boiled for about an hour and a half in the copper, in which soda, in the proportion of a teaspoonful to every two gallons of water, has been dissolved. Some very careful laundresses put the linen into a canvas bag to protect it from the scum and the sides of the copper. When taken out, it should again be rinsed, first in clean hot water, and then in abundance of cold water slightly tinged with fig-blue, and again wrung dry.

It should now be removed from the washing-house and hung up to dry or spread out to bleach, if there are conveniences for it; and the earlier in the day this is done, the clearer and whiter will be the linen. Coloured muslins, cottons, and linens, require a milder treatment; any application of soda will discharge the colour, and soaking all night, even in pure water, deteriorates the more delicate tints. When ready for washing, if not too dirty, they should be put into cold water and washed very speedily, using the common yellow soap, which should be rinsed off immediately.

One article should be washed at a time, and rinsed out immediately before any others are wetted. When washed thoroughly, they should be rinsed in succession in soft water, in which common salt has been dissolved, in the proportion of a handful to three or four gallons, and afterwards wrung gently, as soon as rinsed, with as little twisting as possible, and then hung out to dry. Delicate-coloured articles should not be exposed to the sun, but dried in the shade, using clean lines and wooden pegs.

Woollen articles are liable to shrink, unless the flannel has been well shrunk before making up. This liability is increased where very hot water is used: cold water would thus be the best to wash woollens in; but, as this would not remove the dirt, lukewarm water, about 85°, and yellow soap, are recommended. When thoroughly washed in this, they require a good deal of rinsing in cold water, to remove the soap.

Greasy cloths, which have soaked all night in the liquid described, should be now washed out with soap-and-water as hot as the hands can bear, first in one water, and rinsed out in a second; and afterwards boiled for two hours in water in which a little soda is dissolved. When taken out, they should be rinsed in cold water, and laid out or hung up to dry.

Silk handkerchiefs require to be washed alone. When they contain snuff, they should be soaked by themselves in lukewarm water two or three hours; they should be rinsed out and put to soak with the others in cold water for an hour or two; then washed in lukewarm water, being soaped as they are washed. If this does not remove all stains, they should be washed a second time in similar water, and, when finished, rinsed in soft water in which a handful of common salt has been dissolved. In washing stuff or woollen dresses, the band at the waist and the lining at the bottom should be removed, and wherever it is gathered into folds; and, in furniture, the hems and gatherings.

A black silk dress, if very dirty, must be washed; but, if only soiled, soaking for four-and-twenty hours will do; if old and rusty, a pint of common spirits should be mixed with each gallon of water, which is an improvement under any circumstances. Whether soaked or washed, it should be hung up to drain, and dried without wringing.

Satin and silk ribbons, both white and coloured, may be cleaned in the same manner. Silks, when washed, should be dried in the shade, on a linen-horse, taking care that they are kept smooth and unwrinkled. If black or blue, they will be improved if laid again on the table, when dry, and sponged with gin, or whiskey, or other white spirit.

The operations should be concluded by rinsing the tubs, cleaning the coppers, scrubbing the floors of the washing-house, and restoring everything to order and cleanliness. Thursday and Friday, in a laundry in full employ, are usually devoted to mangling, starching, and ironing. Linen, cotton, and other fabrics, after being washed and dried, are made smooth and glossy by mangling and by ironing.

The mangling process, which is simply passing them between rollers subjected to a very considerable pressure, produced by weight, is confined to sheets, towels, table-linen, and similar articles, which are without folds or plaits. Ironing is necessary to smooth body-linen, and made-up articles of delicate texture or gathered into folds. The mangle is too well known to need description.

Ironing: The irons consist of the common flat-iron, which is of different sizes, varying from 4 to 10 inches in length, triangular in form, and from 2-1/2 to 4-1/2 inches in width at the broad end; the oval iron, which is used for more delicate articles; and the box-iron, which is hollow, and heated by a red-hot iron inserted into the box. The Italian iron is a hollow tube, smooth on the outside, and raised on a slender pedestal with a footstalk. Into the hollow cylinder a red-hot iron is pushed, which heats it; and the smooth outside of the latter is used, on which articles such as frills, and plaited articles, are drawn.

Crimping and gauffering-machines: *Crimping* and gauffering-machines are used for a kind of plaiting where much regularity is required, the articles being passed through two iron rollers fluted so as to represent the kind of plait or fold required.

Starching is a process by which stiffness is communicated to certain parts of linen, as the collar and front of shirts, by dipping them in a paste made of starch boiled in water, mixed with a little gum Arabic, where extra stiffness is required.

Make Starch

Ingredients: Allow 1/2 pint of cold water and 1 quart of boiling water to every 2 tablespoonfuls of starch.

Mode: Put the starch into a tolerably large basin; pour over it the cold water, and stir the mixture well with a wooden spoon until it is perfectly free from lumps, and quite smooth. Then take the basin to the fire, and whilst the water is actually boiling in the kettle or boiler, pour it over the starch, stirring it the whole time. If made properly in this manner, the starch will require no further boiling; but should the water not be boiling when added to the starch, it will not thicken, and must be put into a clean saucepan, and stirred over the fire until it boils. Take it off the fire, strain it into a clean basin, cover it up to prevent a skin forming on the top, and, when sufficiently cool that the hand may be borne in it, starch the things. Many persons, to give a shiny and smooth appearance to the linen when ironed, stir round two or three times in the starch a piece of wax candle, which also prevents the iron from sticking.

When the "things to be starched" are washed, dried, and taken off the lines, they should be dipped into the hot starch made as directed, squeezed out of it, and then just dipped into cold water, and immediately squeezed dry. If fine things be wrung, or roughly used, they are very liable to tear; so too much care cannot be exercised in this respect. If the article is lace, clap it between the hands a few times, which will assist to clear it; then have ready laid out on the table a large clean towel or cloth; shake out the starched things, lay them on the cloth, and roll it up tightly, and let it remain for three or fours, when the things will be ready to iron.

To be able to iron properly requires much practice and experience. Strict cleanliness with all the ironing utensils must be observed, as, if this is not the case, not the most expert ironer will be able to make her things look clear and free from smears, &c. After wiping down her ironing table, the laundry-maid should place a coarse cloth on it, and over that the ironing-blanket, with her stand and iron-rubber; and having ascertained that her irons are quite clean and of the right heat, she proceeds with her work.

It is a good plan to try the heat of the iron on a coarse cloth or apron before ironing anything fine: there is then no danger of scorching. For ironing fine things, such as collars, cuffs, muslins, and laces, there is nothing so clean and nice to use as the box-iron; the bottom being bright, and never placed near the fire, it is always perfectly clean; it should, however, be kept in a dry place, for fear of its rusting. Gauffering-tongs or irons must be placed in a clear fire for a minute, then withdrawn, wiped with a coarse rubber, and the heat of them tried on a piece of paper, as, unless great care is taken, these will very soon scorch.

The skirts of muslin dresses should be ironed on a skirt-board covered with flannel, and the fronts of shirts on a smaller board, also covered with flannel; this board being placed between the back and front. After things are mangled, they should also be ironed in the folds and gathers; dinner-napkins smoothed over, as also table-cloths, pillow-cases, and sometimes sheets. The bands of flannel petticoats, and shoulder-straps to flannel waistcoats, must also undergo the same process.

7

Duties of Nursemaids

The responsible duties of upper nursemaid commence with the weaning of the child: it must now be separated from the mother or wet-nurse, at least for a time, and the cares of the nursemaid, which have hitherto been only occasionally put in requisition, are now to be entirely devoted to the infant. She washes, dresses, and feeds it; walks out with it, and regulates all its little wants; and, even at this early age, many good qualities are required to do so in a satisfactory manner.

Patience and good temper are indispensable qualities; truthfulness, purity of manners, minute cleanliness, and docility and obedience, almost equally so. She ought also to be acquainted with the art of ironing and trimming little caps, and be handy with her needle. There is a considerable art in carrying an infant comfortably for itself and for the nursemaid. If she carry it always seated upright on her arm, and presses it too closely against her chest, the stomach of the child is apt to get compressed, and the back fatigued.

For her own comfort, a good nurse will frequently vary this position, by changing from one arm to the other, and sometimes by laying it across both, raising the head a little. When teaching it to walk, and guiding it by the hand, she should change the hand from time to time, so as to avoid raising one shoulder higher than the other. This is the only way in which a child should be taught to walk; leading-strings and other foolish inventions, which force an infant to make efforts, with its shoulders and head forward, before it knows how to use its limbs, will only render it feeble, and retard its progress.

Most children have some bad habit, of which they must be broken; but this is never accomplished by harshness without developing worse evils: kindness, perseverance, and patience in the nurse, are here of the utmost importance. When finger-sucking is one of these habits, the fingers are sometimes rubbed with bitter aloes, or some equally disagreeable substance. Others have dirty habits, which are only to be changed by patience, perseverance, and, above all, by regularity in the nurse.

She should never be permitted to inflict punishment on these occasions, or, indeed, on any occasion. But, if punishment is to be avoided, it is still more necessary that all kinds of indulgences and flattery be equally forbidden. Yielding to all the whims of a child,– picking up its toys when thrown away in mere wantonness, would be intolerable. A child should never be led to think others inferior to it, to beat a dog, or even the stone against which it falls, as some children are taught to do by silly nurses.

Neither should the nurse affect or show alarm at any of the little accidents which must inevitably happen: if it falls, treat it as a trifle; otherwise she encourages a spirit of cowardice and timidity. But she will take care that such accidents are not of frequent occurrence, or the result of neglect. The nurse should keep the child as clean as possible, and particularly she should train it to habits of cleanliness, so that it should feel uncomfortable when otherwise; watching especially that it does not soil itself in eating.

At the same time, vanity in its personal appearance is not to be encouraged by over-care in this respect, or by too tight lacing or buttoning of dresses, nor a small foot cultivated by the use of tight shoes. Nursemaids would do well to repeat to the parents faithfully and truly the defects they observe in the dispositions of very young children. If properly checked in time, evil propensities may be eradicated; but this should not extend to anything but serious defects; otherwise, the intuitive perceptions which all children possess will construe the act into "spying" and "informing," which should never be resorted to in the case of children, nor, indeed, in any case.

Such are the cares which devolve upon the nursemaid, and it is her duty to fulfil them personally. In large establishments she will have assistants proportioned to the number of children of which she has the care. The under nursemaid lights the fires, sweeps, scours, and dusts the rooms, and makes the beds; empties slops, and carries up water; brings up and removes the nursery meals; washes and dresses all the children, except the infant, and assists in mending. Where there is a nursery girl to assist, she does the rougher part of the cleaning; and all take their meals in the nursery together, after the children of the family have done.

In smaller families, where there is only one nursemaid kept, she is assisted by the housemaid, or servant-of-all-work, who will do the rougher part of the work, and carry up the nursery meals. In such circumstances she will be more immediately under the eye of her mistress, who will probably relieve her from some of the cares of the infant. In higher families, the upper nurse is usually permitted to sup or dine occasionally at the housekeeper's table by way of relaxation, when the children are all well, and her subordinates trustworthy.

Where the nurse has the entire charge of the nursery, and the mother is too much occupied to do more than pay a daily visit to it, it is desirable that she be a person of observation, and possess some acquaintance with the diseases incident to childhood, as also with such simple remedies as may be useful before a medical attendant can be procured, or where such attendance is not considered necessary.

All these little ailments are preceded by symptoms so minute as to be only perceptible to close observation; such as twitching of the brows, restless sleep, grinding the gums, and, in some inflammatory diseases, even to the child abstaining from crying, from fear of the increased pain produced by the movement. Dentition, or cutting the teeth, is attended with many of these symptoms. Measles, thrush, scarlatina, croup, hooping-cough, and other childish complaints, are all preceded by well-known symptoms, which may be alleviated and rendered less virulent by simple remedies instantaneously applied.

Dentition is usually the first serious trouble, bringing many other disorders in its train. The symptoms are most perceptible to the mother: the child sucks feebly, and with gums hot, inflamed, and swollen. In this case, relief is yielded by rubbing them from time to time with a little of Mrs. Johnson's soothing syrup, a valuable and perfectly safe medicine. Selfish and thoughtless nurses, and mothers too, sometimes give cordials and sleeping-draughts, whose effects are too well known.

Convulsion Fits sometimes follow the feverish restlessness produced by these causes; in which case a hot bath should be administered without delay, and the lower parts of the body rubbed, the bath being as hot as it can be without scalding the tender skin; at the same time, the doctor should be sent for immediately, for no nurse should administer medicine in this case, unless the fits have been repeated and the doctor has left directions with her how to act.

Croup is one of the most alarming diseases of childhood; it is accompanied with a hoarse, croaking, ringing cough, and comes on very suddenly, and most so in strong, robust children. A very hot bath should be instantly administered, followed by an emetic, either in the form of tartar-emetic, croup-powder, or a teaspoonful of ipecacuanha, wrapping the body warmly up in flannel after the bath. The slightest delay in administering the bath, or the emetic, may be fatal; hence, the importance of nurses about very young children being acquainted with the symptoms.

Hooping-Cough is generally preceded by the moaning noise during sleep, which even adults threatened with the disorder cannot avoid: it is followed by violent fits of coughing, which little can be done to relieve. A child attacked by this disorder should be kept as much as possible in the fresh, pure air, but out of draughts, and kept warm, and supplied with plenty of nourishing food. Many fatal diseases flow from this scourge of childhood, and a change to purer air, if possible, should follow convalescence.

Worms are the torment of some children: the symptoms are, an unnatural craving for food, even after a full meal; costiveness, suddenly followed by the reverse; fetid breath, a livid circle under the eyes, enlarged abdomen, and picking the nose; for which the remedies must be prescribed by the doctor.

Measles and Scarlatina much resemble each other in their early stages: headache, restlessness, and fretfulness are the symptoms of both. Shivering fits, succeeded by a hot skin; pains in the back and limbs, accompanied by sickness, and, in severe cases, sore throat; pain about the jaws, difficulty in swallowing, running at the eyes, which become red and inflamed, while the face is hot and flushed, often distinguish scarlatina and scarlet fever, of which it is only a mild form.

While the case is doubtful, a dessert-spoonful of spirit of nitre diluted in water, given at bedtime, will throw the child into a gentle perspiration, and will bring out the rash in either case. In measles, this appears first on the face; in scarlatina, on the chest; and in both cases a doctor should be called in. In scarlatina, tartar-emetic powder or ipecacuanha may be administered in the mean time.

In all cases, cleanliness, fresh air, clean utensils, and frequent washing of the person, both of nurse and children, are even more necessary in the nursery than in either drawing-room or sick-room, inasmuch as the delicate organs of childhood are more susceptible of injury from smells and vapours than adults. The duties of a nursemaid, by an extract from Florence Nightingale's admirable "Notes on Nursing." Referring to children, she says:–

"They are much more susceptible than grown people to all noxious influences. They are affected by the same things, but much more quickly and seriously; by want of fresh air, of proper warmth; want of cleanliness in house, clothes, bedding, or body; by improper food, want of punctuality, by dulness, by want of light, by too much or too little covering in bed or when up." And all this in health; and then she quotes a passage from a lecture on sudden deaths in infancy, to show the importance of careful nursing of children:–

"In the great majority of instances, when death suddenly befalls the infant or young child, it is an accident; it is not a necessary, inevitable result of any disease. That which is known to injure children most seriously is foul air; keeping the rooms where they sleep closely shut up is destruction to them; and, if the child's breathing be disordered by disease, a few hours only of such foul air may endanger its life, even where no inconvenience is felt by grown-up persons in the room."

Persons moving in the beat society will see, after perusing Miss Nightingale's book, that this "foul air," "want of light," "too much or too little clothing," and improper food, is not confined to Crown Street or St. Giles's; that Belgravia and the squares have their north room, where the rays of the sun never reach. "A wooden bedstead, two or three mattresses piled up to above the height of the table, a vallance attached to the frame,– nothing but a miracle could ever thoroughly dry or air such a bed and bedding," – is the ordinary bed of a private house, than which nothing can be more unwholesome. "Don't treat your children like sick," she sums up; "don't dose them with tea.

Let them eat meat and drink milk, or half a glass of light beer. Give them fresh, light, sunny, and open rooms, cool bedrooms, plenty of outdoor exercise, facing even the cold, and wind, and weather, in sufficiently warm clothes, and with sufficient exercise, plenty of amusements and play; more liberty, and less schooling, and cramming, and training; more attention to food and less to physic."

Duties of a Sick-nurse

All women are likely, at some period of their lives, to be called on to perform the duties of a sick-nurse, and should prepare themselves as much as possible, by observation and reading, for the occasion when they may be required to perform the office. The main requirements are good temper, compassion for suffering, sympathy with sufferers, which most women worthy of the name possess, neat-handedness, quiet manners, love of order, and cleanliness.

With these qualifications there will be very little to be wished for; the desire to relieve suffering will inspire a thousand little attentions, and surmount the disgusts which some of the offices attending the sick-room are apt to create. Where serious illness visits a household, and protracted nursing is likely to become necessary, a professional nurse will probably be engaged, who has been trained to its duties; but in some families, and those not a few let us hope, the ladies of the family would oppose such an arrangement as a failure of duty on their part.

There is, besides, even when a professional nurse is ultimately called in, a period of doubt and hesitation, while disease has not yet developed itself, when the patient must be attended to; and, in these cases, some of the female servants of the establishment must give their attendance in the sick-room. There are, also, slight attacks of cold, influenza, and accidents in a thousand forms, to which all are subject, where domestic nursing becomes a necessity; where disease, though unattended with danger, is nevertheless accompanied by the nervous irritation incident to illness, and when all the attention of the domestic nurse becomes necessary.

In the first stage of sickness, while doubt and a little perplexity hang over the household as to the nature of the sickness, there are some things about which no doubt can exist: the patient's room must be kept in a perfectly pure state, and arrangements made for proper attendance; for the first canon of nursing, according to Florence Nightingale, its apostle, is to "keep the air the patient breathes as pure as the external air, without chilling him." This can be done without any preparation which might alarm the patient; with proper windows, open fireplaces, and a supply of fuel, the room may be as fresh as it is outside, and kept at a temperature suitable for the patient's state.

Windows, however, must be opened from above, and not from below, and draughts avoided; cool air admitted beneath the patient's head chills the lower strata and the floor. The careful nurse will keep the door shut when the window is open; she will also take care that the patient is not placed between the door and the open window, nor between the open fireplace and the window. If confined to bed, she will see that the bed is placed in a thoroughly ventilated part of the room, but out of the current of air which is produced by the momentary opening of doors, as well as out of the line of draught between the window and the open chimney, and that the temperature of the room is kept about 64°.

Where it is necessary to admit air by the door, the windows should be closed; but there are few circumstances in which good air can be obtained through the chamber-door; through it, on the contrary, the gases generated in the lower parts of the house are likely to be drawn into the invalid chamber. These precautions taken, and plain nourishing diet, such as the patient desires, furnished, probably little more can be done, unless more serious symptoms present themselves; in which case medical advice will be sought.

Under no circumstances is ventilation of the sick-room so essential as in cases of febrile diseases, usually considered infectious; such as typhus and puerperal fevers, influenza, hooping-cough, small — and chicken-pox, scarlet fever, measles, and erysipelas: all these are considered communicable through the air; but there is little danger of infection being thus communicated, provided the room is kept thoroughly ventilated. On the contrary, if this essential be neglected, the power of infection is greatly increased and concentrated in the confined and impure air; it settles upon the clothes of the attendants and visitors, especially where they are of wool, and is frequently communicated to other families in this manner.

Under all circumstances, therefore, the sick-room should be kept as fresh and sweet as the open air, while the temperature is kept up by artificial heat, taking care that the fire burns clear, and gives out no smoke into the room; that the room is perfectly clean, wiped over with a damp cloth every day, if boarded; and swept, after sprinkling with damp tea-leaves, or other aromatic leaves, if carpeted; that all utensils are emptied and cleaned as soon as used, and not once in four-and-twenty hours, as is sometimes done.

"A slop-pail," Miss Nightingale says, "should never enter a sick-room; everything should be carried direct to the water-closet, emptied there, and brought up clean; in the best hospitals the slop-pail is unknown." "I do not approve," says Miss Nightingale, "of making housemaids of nurses,— that would be waste of means; but I have seen surgical sisters, women whose hands were worth to them two or three guineas a week, down on their knees, scouring a room or hut, because they thought it was not fit for their patients: these women had the true nurse spirit."

Bad smells are sometimes met by sprinkling a little liquid chloride of lime on the floor; fumigation by burning pastiles is also a common expedient for the purification of the sick-room. They are useful, but only in the sense hinted at by the medical lecturer, who commenced his lecture thus:— "Fumigations, gentlemen, are of essential importance; they make so abominable a smell, that they compel you to open the windows and admit fresh air." In this sense they are useful, but ineffectual unless the cause be removed, and fresh air admitted.

The sick-room should be quiet; no talking, no gossiping, and, above all, no whispering,— this is absolute cruelty to the patient; he thinks his complaint the subject, and strains his ear painfully to catch the sound. No rustling of dresses, nor creaking shoes either; where the carpets are taken up, the nurse should wear list shoes, or some other noiseless material, and her dress should be of soft material that does not rustle. Miss Nightingale denounces crinoline, and quotes Lord Melbourne on the subject of women in the sick-room, who said, "I would rather have men about me, when ill, than women; it requires very strong health to put up with women." Ungrateful man! but absolute quiet is necessary in the sick-room.

Never let the patient be waked out of his first sleep by noise, never roused by anything like a surprise. Always sit in the apartment, so that the patient has you in view, and that it is not necessary for him to turn in speaking to you. Never keep a patient standing; never speak to one while moving. Never lean on the sick-bed. Above all, be calm and decisive with the patient, and prevent all noises over-head. A careful nurse, when a patient leaves his bed, will open the sheets wide, and throw the clothes back so as thoroughly to air the bed; She will avoid drying or airing anything damp in the sick-room.

"It is another fallacy," says Florence Nightingale, "to suppose that night air is injurious; a great authority told me that, in London, the air is never so good as after ten o'clock, when smoke has diminished; but then it must be air from without, not within, and not air vitiated by gaseous airs." "A great fallacy prevails also," she says, in another section, "about flowers poisoning the air of the sick-room: no one ever saw them over-crowding the sick-room; but, if they did, they actually absorb carbonic acid and give off oxygen."

Cut flowers also decompose water, and produce oxygen gas. Lilies, and some other very odorous plants, may perhaps give out smells unsuited to a close room, while the atmosphere of the sick-room should always be fresh and natural. "Patients," says Miss Nightingale, "are sometimes starved in the midst of plenty, from want of attention to the ways which alone make it possible for them to take food. A spoonful of beef-tea, or arrowroot and wine, or some other light nourishing diet, should be given every hour, for the patient's stomach will reject large supplies.

In very weak patients there is often a nervous difficulty in swallowing, which is much increased if food is not ready and presented at the moment when it is wanted: the nurse should be able to discriminate, and know when this moment is approaching." Diet suitable for patients will depend, in some degree, on their natural likes and dislikes, which the nurse will do well to acquaint herself with. Beef-tea is useful and relishing, but possesses little nourishment; when evaporated, it presents a teaspoonful of solid meat to a pint of water.

Eggs are not equivalent to the same weight of meat. Arrowroot is less nourishing than flour. Butter is the lightest and most digestible kind of fat. Cream, in some diseases, cannot be replaced. But, to sum up with some of Miss Nightingale's useful maxims:– Observation is the nurse's best guide, and the patient's appetite the rule. Half a pint of milk is equal to a quarter of a pound of meat. Beef-tea is the least nourishing food administered to the sick; and tea and coffee, she thinks, are both too much excluded from the sick-room.

Monthly Nurse

The choice of a monthly nurse is of the utmost importance; and in the case of a young mother with her first child, it would be well for her to seek advice and counsel from her more experienced relatives in this matter. In the first place, the engaging a monthly nurse in good time is of the utmost importance, as, if she be competent and clever, her services will be sought months beforehand; a good nurse having seldom much of her time disengaged.

There are some qualifications which it is evident the nurse should possess: she should be scrupulously clean and tidy in her person; honest, sober, and noiseless in her movements; should possess a natural love for children, and have a strong nerve in case of emergencies. Snuff-taking and spirit-drinking must not be included in her habits; but these are happily much less frequent than they were in former days.

Receiving, as she often will, instructions from the doctor, she should bear these in mind, and carefully carry them out. In those instances where she does not feel herself sufficiently informed, she should ask advice from the medical man, and not take upon herself to administer medicines, &c., without his knowledge. A monthly nurse should be between 30 and 50 years of age, sufficiently old to have had a little experience, and yet not too old or infirm to be able to perform various duties requiring strength and bodily vigour.

She should be able to wake the moment she is called, – at any hour of the night, that the mother or child may have their wants immediately attended to. Good temper, united to a kind and gentle disposition, is indispensable; and, although the nurse will frequently have much to endure from the whims and caprices of the invalid, she should make allowances for these, and command her temper, at the same time exerting her authority when it is necessary.

What the nurse has to do in the way of cleaning and dusting her lady's room, depends entirely on the establishment that is kept. Where there are plenty of servants, the nurse, of course, has nothing whatever to do but attend on her patient, and ring the bell for anything she may require. Where the number of domestics is limited, she should not mind keeping her room in order; that is to say, sweeping and dusting it every morning. If fires be necessary, the housemaid should always clean the grate, and do all that is wanted in that way, as this, being rather dirty work, would soil the nurse's dress, and unfit her to approach the bed, or take the infant without soiling its clothes.

In small establishments, too, the nurse should herself fetch things she may require, and not ring every time she wants anything; and she must, of course, not leave her invalid unless she sees everything is comfortable; and then only for a few minutes. When down stairs, and in company with the other servants, the nurse should not repeat what she may have heard in her lady's room, as much mischief may be done by a gossiping nurse. As in most houses the monthly nurse is usually sent for a few days before her services may be required, she should see that all is in readiness; that there be no bustle and hurry at the time the confinement takes place.

She should keep two pairs of sheets thoroughly aired, as well as night-dresses, flannels, &c. &c. All the things which will be required to dress the baby the first time should be laid in the basket in readiness, in the order in which they are to be put on; as well as scissors, thread, a few pieces of soft linen rag, and two or three flannel squares. If a berceaunette is to be used immediately, the nurse should ascertain that the mattresses, pillow, &c. are all well aired; and if not already done before she arrives, she should assist in covering and trimming it, ready for the little occupant.

A monthly nurse should be handy at her needle, as, if she is in the house some time before the baby is born, she will require some work of this sort; to occupy her time. She should also understand the making-up of little caps, although we can scarcely say this is one of the nurse's duties. As most children wear no caps, except out of doors, her powers in this way will not be much taxed.

A nurse should endeavour to make her room as cheerful as possible, and always keep it clean and tidy. She should empty the chamber utensils as soon as used, and on no account put things under the bed. Soiled baby's napkins should be rolled up and put into a pan, when they should be washed out every morning, and hung out to dry: they are then in a fit state to send to the laundress; and should, on no account, be left dirty, but done every morning in this way. The bedroom should be kept rather dark, particularly for the first week or ten days; of a regular temperature, and as free as possible from draughts, at the same time well ventilated and free from unpleasant smells.

The infant during the month must not be exposed to strong light, or much air; and in carrying it about the passages, stairs, &c., the nurse should always have its head-flannel on, to protect the eyes and ears from the currents of air. For the management of children, we must refer our readers to the following chapters; and we need only say, in conclusion, that a good nurse should understand the symptoms of various ills incident to this period, as, in all cases, prevention is better than cure.

As young mothers with their first baby are very often much troubled at first with their breasts, the nurse should understand the art of emptying them by suction, or some other contrivance. If the breasts are kept well drawn, there will be but little danger of inflammation; and as the infant at first cannot take all that is necessary, something must be done to keep the inflammation down. This is one of the greatest difficulties a nurse has to contend with, and we can only advise her to be very persevering, to rub the breasts well, and to let the infant suck as soon and as often as possible, until they get in proper order.

Wet Nurse

We are aware that, according to the opinion of some ladies, there is no domestic theme, during a certain period of their married lives, more fraught with vexation and disquietude than that ever-fruitful source of annoyance, "the Nurse;" but, there are thousands of excellent wives and mothers who pass through life without even a temporary embroglio in the kitchen, or suffering a state of moral hectic the whole time of a nurse's empire in the nursery or bedroom.

Our own experience goes to prove, that although many unqualified persons palm themselves off on ladies as fully competent for the duties they so rashly and dishonestly undertake to perform, and thus expose themselves to ill-will and merited censure, there are still very many fully equal to the legitimate exercise of what they undertake; and if they do not in every case give entire satisfaction, some of the fault,– and sometimes a great deal of it,– may be honestly placed to the account of the ladies themselves, who, in many instances, are so impressed with the propriety of their own method of performing everything, as to insist upon the adoption of their system in preference to that of the nurse, whose plan is probably based on a comprehensive forethought, and rendered perfect in all its details by an ample experience.

In all our remarks on this subject, we should remember with gentleness the order of society from which our nurses are drawn; and that those who make their duty a study, and are termed professional nurses, have much to endure from the caprice and egotism of their employers; while others are driven to the occupation from the laudable motive of feeding their own children, and who, in fulfilling that object, are too often both selfish and sensual, performing, without further interest than is consistent with their own advantage, the routine of customary duties.

Properly speaking, there are two nurses,– the nurse for the mother and the nurse for the child, or, the monthly and the wet nurse. Of the former we have already spoken, and will now proceed to describe the duties of the latter, and add some suggestions as to her age, physical health, and moral conduct, subjects of the utmost importance as far as the charge intrusted to her is concerned, and therefore demanding some special remarks.

When from illness, suppression of the milk, accident, or some natural process, the mother is deprived of the pleasure of rearing her infant, it becomes necessary at once to look around for a fitting substitute, so that the child may not suffer, by any needless delay, a physical loss by the deprivation of its natural food. The first consideration should be as regards age, state of health, and temper.

The age, if possible, should not be less than twenty nor exceed thirty years, with the health sound in every respect, and the body free from all eruptive disease or local blemish. The best evidence of a sound state of health will be found in the woman's clear open countenance, the ruddy tone of the skin, the full, round, and elastic state of the breasts, and especially in the erectile, firm condition of the nipple, which, in all unhealthy states of the body, is pendulous, flabby, and relaxed; in which case, the milk is sure to be imperfect in its organization, and, consequently, deficient in its nutrient qualities.

Appetite is another indication of health in the suckling nurse or mother; for it is impossible a woman can feed her child without having a corresponding appetite; and though inordinate craving for food is neither desirable nor necessary, a natural vigour should be experienced at meal-times, and the food taken should be anticipated and enjoyed.

Besides her health, the moral state of the nurse is to be taken into account, or that mental discipline or principle of conduct which would deter the nurse from at any time gratifying her own pleasures and appetites at the cost or suffering of her infant charge. The conscientiousness and good faith that would prevent a nurse so acting are, unfortunately, very rare; and many nurses, rather than forego the enjoyment of a favourite dish, though morally certain of the effect it will have on the child, will, on the first opportunity, feed with avidity on fried meats, cabbage, cucumbers, pickles, or other crude and injurious aliments, in defiance of all orders given, or confidence reposed in their word, good sense, and humanity.

And when the infant is afterwards racked with pain, and a night of disquiet alarms the mother, the doctor is sent for, and the nurse, covering her dereliction by a falsehood, the consequence of her gluttony is treated as a disease, and the poor infant is dosed for some days with medicines, that can do it but little if any good, and, in all probability, materially retard its physical development.

The selfish nurse, in her ignorance, believes, too, that as long as she experiences no admonitory symptoms herself, the child cannot suffer; and satisfied that, whatever is the cause of its screams and plunges, neither she, nor what she had eaten, had anything to do with it, with this flattering assurance at her heart, she watches her opportunity, and has another luxurious feast off the proscribed dainties, till the increasing disturbance in the child's health, or treachery from the kitchen, opens the eyes of mother and doctor to the nurse's unprincipled conduct.

In all such cases the infant should be spared the infliction of medicine, and, as a wholesome corrective to herself, and relief to her charge, a good sound dose administered to the nurse. Respecting the diet of the wet-nurse, the first point of importance is to fix early and definite hours for every meal; and the mother should see that no cause is ever allowed to interfere with their punctuality. The food itself should be light, easy of digestion, and simple.

Boiled or roast meat, with bread and potatoes, with occasionally a piece of sago, rice, or tapioca pudding, should constitute the dinner, the only meal that requires special comment; broths, green vegetables, and all acid or salt foods, must be avoided. Fresh fish, once or twice a week, may be taken; but it is hardly sufficiently nutritious to be often used as a meal. If the dinner is taken early,–

at one o'clock,– there will be no occasion for luncheon, which too often, to the injury of the child, is made the cover for a first dinner.

Half a pint of stout, with a Reading biscuit, at eleven o'clock, will be abundantly sufficient between breakfast at eight and a good dinner, with a pint of porter at one o'clock. About eight o'clock in the evening, half a pint of stout, with another biscuit, may be taken; and for supper, at ten or half-past, a pint of porter, with a slice of toast or a small amount of bread and cheese, may conclude the feeding for the day.

Animal food once in twenty-four hours is quite sufficient. All spirits, unless in extreme cases, should be avoided; and wine is still more seldom needed. With a due quantity of plain digestible food, and the proportion of stout and porter ordered, with early hours and regularity, the nurse will not only be strong and healthy herself, but fully capable of rearing a child in health and strength.

There are two points all mothers, who are obliged to employ wet-nurses, should remember, and be on their guard against. The first is, never to allow a nurse to give medicine to the infant on her own authority: many have such an infatuated idea of the healing excellence of castor-oil, that they would administer a dose of this disgusting grease twice a week, and think they had done a meritorious service to the child.

The next point is, to watch carefully, lest, to insure a night's sleep for herself, she does not dose the infant with Godfrey's cordial, syrup of poppies, or some narcotic potion, to insure tranquillity to the one and give the opportunity of sleep to the other. The fact that scores of nurses keep secret bottles of these deadly syrups, for the purpose of stilling their charges, is notorious; and that many use them to a fearful extent, is sufficiently patent to all.

It therefore behoves the mother, while obliged to trust to a nurse, to use her best discretion to guard her child from the unprincipled treatment of the person she must, to a certain extent, depend upon and trust; and to remember, in all cases, rather than resort to castor-oil or sedatives, to consult a medical man for her infant in preference to following the counsel of her nurse.

Duties of Lady's-maid

The duties of a lady's-maid are more numerous, and perhaps more onerous, than those of the valet; for while the latter is aided by the tailor, the hatter, the linen-draper, and the perfumer, the lady's-maid has to originate many parts of the mistress's dress herself: she should, indeed, be a tolerably expert milliner and dressmaker, a good hairdresser, and possess some chemical knowledge of the cosmetics with which the toilet-table is supplied, in order to use them with safety and effect.

Her first duty in the morning, after having performed her own toilet, is to examine the clothes put off by her mistress the evening before, either to put them away, or to see that they are all in order to put on again. During the winter, and in wet weather, the dresses should be carefully examined, and the mud removed. Dresses of tweed, and other woollen materials, may be laid out on a table and brushed all over; but in general, even in woollen fabrics, the lightness of the tissues renders brushing unsuitable to dresses, and it is better to remove the dust from the folds by beating them lightly with a handkerchief or thin cloth.

Silk dresses should never be brushed, but rubbed with a piece of merino, or other soft material, of a similar colour, kept for the purpose. Summer dresses of barège, muslin, mohair, and other light materials, simply require shaking; but if the muslin be tumbled, it must be ironed afterwards. If the dresses require slight repair, it should be done at once: "a stitch in time saves nine." The bonnet should be dusted with a light feather plume, in order to remove every particle of dust; but this has probably been done, as it ought to have been, the night before. Velvet bonnets, and other velvet articles of dress, should be cleaned with a soft brush.

If the flowers with which the bonnet is decorated have been crushed or displaced, or the leaves tumbled, they should be raised and readjusted by means of flower-pliers. If feathers have suffered from damp, they should be held near the fire for a few minutes, and restored to their natural state by the hand or a soft brush. The Chausserie, or foot-gear of a lady, is one of the few things left to mark her station, and requires special care. Satin boots or shoes should be dusted with a soft brush, or wiped with a cloth.

Kid or varnished leather should have the mud wiped off with a sponge charged with milk, which preserves its softness and polish. The following is also an excellent polish for applying to ladies' boots, instead of blacking them:– Mix equal proportions of sweet-oil, vinegar, and treacle, with 1 oz. of lamp-black. When all the ingredients are thoroughly incorporated, rub the mixture on the boots with the palm of the hand, and put them in a cool place to dry. Ladies' blacking, which may be purchased in 6d, and 1s. bottles, is also very much used for patent leather and kid boots, particularly when they are a little worn.

This blacking is merely applied with a piece of sponge, and the boots should not be put on until the blacking is dry und hardened. These various preliminary offices performed, the lady's-maid should prepare for dressing her mistress, arranging her dressing-room, toilet-table, and linen, according to her mistress's wishes and habits. The details of dressing we need not touch upon, – every lady has her own mode of doing so; but the maid should move about quietly, perform any offices about her mistress's person, as lacing stays, gently, and adjust her linen smoothly.

Having prepared the dressing-room by lighting the fire, sweeping the hearth, and made everything ready for dressing her mistress, placed her linen before the fire to air, and laid out the various articles of dress she is to wear, which will probably have been arranged the previous evening, the lady's-maid is prepared for the morning's duties. Hairdressing is the most important part of the lady's-maid's office. If ringlets are worn, remove the curl-papers, and, after thoroughly brushing the back hair both above and below, dress it according to the prevailing fashion.

If bandeaux are worn, the hair is thoroughly brushed and frizzed outside and inside, folding the hair back round the head, brushing it perfectly smooth, giving it a glossy appearance by the use of pomades, or oil, applied by the palm of the hand, smoothing it down with a small brush dipped in bandoline. Double bandeaux are formed by bringing most of the hair forward, and rolling it over frizettes made of hair the same colour as that of the wearer: it is finished behind by plaiting the hair, and arranging it in such a manner as to look well with the head-dress.

Lessons in hairdressing may be obtained, and at not an unreasonable charge. If a lady's-maid can afford it, we would advise her to initiate herself in the mysteries of hairdressing before entering on her duties. If a mistress finds her maid handy, and willing to learn, she will not mind the expense of a few lessons, which are almost necessary, as the fashion and mode of dressing the hair is so continually changing. Brushes and combs should be kept scrupulously clean, by washing them about twice a week: to do this oftener spoils the brushes, as very frequent washing makes them so very soft.

Wash Brushes

Dissolve a piece of soda in some hot water, allowing a piece the size of a walnut to a quart of water. Put the water into a basin, and, after combing out the hair from the brushes, dip them, bristles downwards, into the water and out again, keeping the backs and handles as free from the water as possible. Repeat this until the bristles look clean; then rinse the brushes in a little cold water; shake them well, and wipe the handles and backs with a towel, but not the bristles, and set the brushes to dry in the sun, or near the fire; but take care not to put them too close to it. Wiping the bristles of a brush makes them soft, as does also the use of soap.

Clean Combs

If it can be avoided, never wash combs, as the water often makes the teeth split, and the tortoiseshell or horn of which they are made, rough. Small brushes, manufactured purposely for cleaning combs, may be purchased at a trifling cost: with this the comb should be well brushed, and afterwards wiped with a cloth or towel.

Good Wash for Hair

Ingredients: 1 pennyworth of borax, 1/2 pint of olive-oil, 1 pint of boiling water.

Mode: Pour the boiling water over the borax and oil; let it cool; then put the mixture into a bottle. Shake it before using, and apply it with a flannel. Camphor and borax, dissolved in boiling water and left to cool, make a very good wash for the hair; as also does rosemary-water mixed with a little borax. After using any of these washes, when the hair becomes thoroughly dry, a little pomatum or oil should be rubbed in, to make it smooth and glossy.

Make Pomade for Hair

Ingredients: 1/4 lb. of lard, 2 pennyworth of castor-oil; scent.

Mode: Let the lard be unsalted; beat it up well; then add the castor-oil, and mix thoroughly together with a knife, adding a few drops of any scent that may be preferred. Put the pomatum into pots, which keep well covered to prevent it turning rancid.

Pomatum

Ingredients: 8 oz. of olive-oil, 1 oz. of spermaceti, 3 pennyworth of essential oil of almonds, 3 pennyworth of essence of lemon.

Mode: Mix these ingredients together, and store away in jars for use.

To make Bandoline

Ingredients: 1 oz. of gum-tragacanth, 1/4 pint of cold water, 3 pennyworth of essence of almonds, 2 teaspoonfuls of old rum.

Mode: Put the gum-tragacanth into a wide-mouthed bottle with the cold water; let it stand till dissolved, then stir into it the essence of almonds; let it remain for an hour or two, when pour the rum on the top. This should make the stock bottle, and when any is required for use, it is merely necessary to dilute it with a little cold water until the desired consistency is obtained, and to keep it in a small bottle, well corked, for use. This bandoline, instead of injuring the hair, as many other kinds often do, improves it, by increasing its growth, and making it always smooth and glossy.

Excellent Pomatum

Ingredients: 1-1/2 lb. of lard, 1/2 pint of olive-oil, 1/2 pint of castor-oil, 4 oz. of spermaceti, bergamot, or any other scent; elder-flower water.

Mode: Wash the lard well in the elder-flower water; drain, and beat it to a cream. Mix the two oils together, and heat them sufficiently to dissolve the spermaceti, which should be beaten fine in a mortar. Mix all these ingredients together with the brandy and whatever kind of scent may be preferred; and whilst warm pour into glass bottles for use, keeping them well corked. The best way to liquefy the pomatum is to set the bottle in a saucepan of warm water. It will remain good for many months.

Promote Growth of Hair

Ingredients: Equal quantities of olive-oil and spirit of rosemary; a few drops of oil of nutmeg.

Mode: Mix the ingredients together, rub the roots of the hair every night with a little of this liniment, and the growth of it will very soon sensibly increase.

Our further remarks on dressing must be confined to some general advice. In putting on a band, see that it is laid quite flat, and is drawn tightly round the waist before it is pinned in front; that the pin is a strong one, and that it is secured to the stays, so as not to slip up or down, or crease in the folds. Arrange the folds of the dress over the crinoline petticoats; if the dress fastens behind, put a small pin in the slit to prevent it from opening. See that the sleeves fall well over the arms.

If it is finished with a jacket, or other upper dress, see that it fits smoothly under the arms; pull out the flounces, and spread out the petticoat at the bottom with the hands, so that it falls in graceful folds. In arranging the petticoat itself, a careful lady's-maid will see that this is firmly fastened round the waist.

Where sashes are worn, pin the bows securely on the inside with a pin, so as not to be visible; then raise the bow with the fingers. The collar is arranged and carefully adjusted with brooch or bow in the centre. Having dressed her mistress for breakfast, and breakfasted herself, the further duties of the lady's-maid will depend altogether upon the habits of the family, in which hardly two will probably agree.

Where the duties are entirely confined to attendance on her mistress, it is probable that the bedroom and dressing-room will be committed to her care; that, the housemaid will rarely enter, except for the weekly or other periodical cleaning; she will, therefore, have to make her mistress's bed, and keep it in order; and as her duties are light and easy, there can be no allowance made for the slightest approach to uncleanliness or want of order.

Every morning, immediately after her mistress has left it, and while breakfast is on, she should throw the bed open, by taking off the clothes; open the windows, and leave the room to air for half an hour. After breakfast, except her attendance on her mistress prevents it, if the rooms are carpeted, she should sweep them carefully, having previously strewed the room with moist tea-leaves, dusting every table and chair, taking care to penetrate to every corner, and moving every article of furniture that is portable.

This done satisfactorily, and having cleaned the dressing-glass, polished up the furniture and the ornaments, and made the glass jug and basin clean and bright, emptied all slops, emptied the water-jugs and filled them with fresh water, and arranged the rooms, the dressing-room is ready for the mistress when she thinks proper to appear. The dressing-room thoroughly in order, the same thing is to be done in the bedroom, in which she will probably be assisted by the housemaid to make the bed and empty the slops.

In making the bed, she will study her lady's wishes, whether it is to be hard or soft, sloping or straight, and see that it is done accordingly. Having swept the bedroom with equal care, dusted the tables and chairs, chimney-ornaments, and put away all articles of dress left from yesterday, and cleaned and put away any articles of jewellery, her next care is to see, before her mistress goes out, what requires replacing in her department, and furnish her with a list of them, that she may use her discretion about ordering them. All this done, she may settle herself down to any work on which she is engaged.

This will consist chiefly in mending; which is first to be seen to; everything, except stockings, being mended before washing. Plain work will probably be one of the lady's-maid's chief employments. A waiting-maid, who wishes to make herself useful, will study the fashion-books with attention, so as to be able to aid her mistress's judgment in dressing, according to the prevailing fashion, with such modifications as her style of countenance requires.

She will also, if she has her mistress's interest at heart, employ her spare time in repairing and making up dresses which have served one purpose, to serve another also, or turning many things, unfitted for her mistress to use, for the younger branches of the family. The lady's-maid may thus render herself invaluable to her mistress, and increase her own happiness in so doing. The exigencies of fashion and luxury are such, that all ladies, except those of the very highest rank, will consider themselves fortunate in having about them a thoughtful person, capable of diverting their finery to a useful purpose.

Among other duties, the lady's-maid should understand the various processes for washing, and cleaning, and repairing laces; edging of collars; removing stains and grease-spots from dresses, and similar processes, for which the following recipes will be found very useful. Blonde, fine toilet-soap is used; the blonde is soaped over very slightly, and washed in water in which a little fig-blue is dissolved, rubbing it very gently; when clean, dry it.

Dip it afterwards in very thin gum-water, dry it again in linen, spread it out as flat as it will lie, and iron it. Where the blonde is of better quality, and wider, it may be stretched on a hoop to dry after washing in the blue-water, applying the gum with a sponge; or it may be washed finally in water in which a lump of sugar has been dissolved, which gives it more the appearance of new blonde.

Lace collars soil very quickly when in contact with the neck; they are cleaned by beating the edge of the collar between the folds of a fine linen cloth, then washing the edges as directed above, and spreading it out on an ironing-board, pinning it at each corner with fine pins; then going carefully over it with a sponge charged with water in which some gum-dragon and fig-blue have been dissolved, to give it a proper consistence. To give the collar the same tint throughout, the whole collar should be sponged with the same water, taking care not to touch the flowers.

Grease-spots from cotton or woollen materials of fast colours, absorbent pastes, purified bullock's-blood, and even common soap, are used, applied to the spot when dry. When the colours are not fast, use fuller's-earth or pulverized potter's-clay, laid in a layer over the spot, and press it with a very hot iron. For Silks, Moires, and plain or brocaded Satins, begin by pouring over the spot two drops of rectified spirits of wine; cover it over with a linen cloth, and press it with a hot iron, changing the linen instantly.

The spot will look tarnished, for a portion of the grease still remains: this will be removed entirely by a little sulphuric ether dropped on the spot, and a very little rubbing. If neatly done, no perceptible mark or circle will remain; nor will the lustre of the richest silk be changed, the union of the two liquids operating with no injurious effects from rubbing. Fruit-spots are removed from white and fast-coloured cottons by the use of chloride of soda.

Commence by cold-soaping the article, then touch the spot with a hair-pencil or feather dipped in the chloride, dipping it immediately into cold water, to prevent the texture of the article being injured. Ink-spots are removed, when fresh applied to the spot, by a few drops of hot water being poured on immediately afterwards. By the same process, iron-mould in linen or calico may be removed, dipping immediately in cold water to prevent injury to the fabric.

Wax dropped on a shawl, table-cover, or cloth dress, is easily discharged by applying spirits of wine. Syrups or Preserved Fruits, by washing in lukewarm water with a dry cloth, and pressing the spot between two folds of clean linen. Essence of Lemon will remove grease, but will make a spot itself in a few days.

Clean Silk or Ribbons

Ingredients: 1/2 pint of gin, 1/2 lb. of honey, 1/2 lb. of soft soap, 1/2 pint of water.

Mode: Mix the above ingredients together; then lay each breadth of silk upon a clean kitchen table or dresser, and scrub it well on the soiled side with the mixture. Have ready three vessels of cold water; take each piece of silk at two corners, and dip it up and down in each vessel, but do not wring it; and take care that each breadth has one vessel of quite clean water for the last dip. Hang it up dripping for a minute or two, then dab it in a cloth, and iron it quickly with a very hot iron.

Remove Paint-spots from Silk Cloth

If the fabric will bear it, sharp rubbing will frequently entirely discharge a newly-made paint-stain; but, if this is not successful, apply spirit of turpentine with a quill till the stains disappear.

To make old Crape look nearly equal to new. Place a little water in a teakettle, and let it boil until there is plenty of steam from the spout; then, holding the crape in both hands, pass it to and fro several times through the steam, and it will to clean and look nearly equal to new.

Linen: Before sending linen to wash, the lady's-maid should see that everything under her charge is properly mended; for her own sake she should take care that it is sent out in an orderly manner, each class of garments by themselves, with a proper list, of which she retains a copy. On its return, it is still more necessary to examine every piece separately, so that all missing buttons be supplied, and only the articles properly washed and in perfect repair passed into the wardrobe.

Ladies who keep a waiting-maid for their own persons are in the habit of paying visits to their friends, in which it is not unusual for the maid to accompany them; at all events, it is her duty to pack the trunks; and this requires not only knowledge but some practice, although the improved trunks and portmanteaus now made, in which there is a place for nearly everything, render this more simple than formerly. Before packing, let the trunks be thoroughly well cleaned, and, if necessary, lined with paper, and everything intended for packing laid out on the bed or chairs, so that it may be seen what is to be stowed away; the nicer articles of dress neatly folded in clean calico wrappers.

Having satisfied herself that everything wanted is laid out, and that it is in perfect order, the packing is commenced by disposing of the most bulky articles, the dressing-case and work-box, skirts, and other articles requiring room, leaving the smaller articles to fill up; finally, having satisfied herself that all is included, she should lock and cover up the trunk in its canvas case, and then pack her own box, if she is to accompany her mistress.

On reaching the house, the lady's-maid will be shown her lady's apartment; and her duties here are what they were at home; she will arrange her mistress's things, and learn which is her bell, in order to go to her when she rings. Her meals will be taken in the housekeeper's room; and here she must be discreet and guarded in her talk to any one of her mistress or her concerns. Her only occupation here will be attending in her lady's room, keeping her things in order, and making her rooms comfortable for her.

The evening duties of a lady's-maid are pretty nearly a repetition of those of the morning. She is in attendance when her mistress retires; she assists her to undress if required, brushes her hair, and renders such other assistance as is demanded; removes all slops; takes care that the fire, if any, is safe, before she retires to rest herself. Ironing is a part of the duties of a lady's-maid, and she should be able to do it in the most perfect manner when it becomes necessary.

Ironing is often badly done from inattention to a few very simple requirements. Cleanliness is the first essential: the ironing-board, the fire, the iron, and the ironing-blanket should all be perfectly clean. It will not be necessary here to enter into details on ironing, as full directions are given in the "Duties of the Laundry-maid." A lady's-maid will have a great deal of "Ironing-out" to do; such as light evening dresses, muslin dresses, &c., which are not dirty enough to be washed, but merely require smoothing out to remove the creases.

In summer, particularly, an iron will be constantly required, as also a skirt-board, which should be covered with a nice clean piece of flannel. To keep muslin dresses in order, they almost require smoothing out every time they are worn, particularly if made with many flounces. The lady's-maid may often have to perform little services for her mistress which require care; such as restoring the colour to scorched linen, &c. &c. The following recipe is a very good one.

Restore Whiteness to Scorched Linen

Ingredients: 1/2 pint of vinegar, 2 oz. of fuller's-earth, 1 oz. of dried fowls' dung, 1/2 oz. of soap, the juice of 2 large onions.

Mode: Boil all these ingredients together to the consistency of paste; spread the composition thickly over the damaged part, and if the threads be not actually consumed, after it has been allowed to dry on, and the place has subsequently been washed once or twice, every trace of scorching will disappear.

Furs, Feathers, and Woollens require the constant care of the waiting-maid. Furs and feathers not in constant use should be wrapped up in linen washed in lye. From May to September they are subject to being made the depositary of the moth-eggs. They should be looked too, and shaken and beaten, from time to time, in case some of the eggs should have been lodged in them, in spite of every precaution; laying them up again, or rather folding them up as before, wrapping them in brown paper, which is itself a preservative. Shawls and cloaks, which would be damaged by such close folds, must be looked to, and aired and beaten, putting them away dry before the evening.

Ravages of Moths

Place pieces of camphor, cedar-wood, Russia leather, tobacco-leaves, bog-myrtle, or anything else strongly aromatic, in the drawers or boxes where furs or other things to be preserved from moths are kept, and they will never take harm.

Jewels are generally wrapped up in cotton, and kept in their cases; but they are subject to tarnish from exposure to the air, and require cleaning. This is done by preparing clean soap-suds, using fine toilet-soap. Dip any article of gold, silver, gilt, or precious stones into this lye, and dry them by brushing with a brush of soft badgers' hair, or a fine sponge; afterwards with a piece of fine cloth, and, lastly, with a soft leather.

Epaulettes of gold or silver, and, in general, all articles of jewellery, may be dressed by dipping them in spirits of wine warmed in a bain marie, or shallow kettle, placed over a slow fire or hot-plate. The valet and lady's-maid, from their supposed influence with their master and mistress, are exposed to some temptations to which other servants are less subjected. They are probably in communication with the tradespeople who supply articles for the toilet; such as batters, tailors, dressmakers, and perfumers.

The conduct of waiting-maid and valet to these people should be civil but independent, making reasonable allowance for want of exact punctuality, if any such can be made: they should represent any inconvenience respectfully, and if an excuse seems unreasonable, put the matter fairly to master or mistress, leaving it to them to notice it further, if they think it necessary. No expectations of a personal character should influence them one way or the other.

It would be acting unreasonably to any domestic to make them refuse such presents as tradespeople choose to give them; the utmost that can be expected is that they should not influence their judgment in the articles supplied — that they should represent them truly to master or mistress, without fear and without favour. Civility to all, servility to none, is a good maxim for every one. Deference to a master and mistress, and to their friends and visitors, is one of the implied terms of their engagement; and this deference must apply even to what may be considered their whims.

A servant is not to be seated, or wear a hat in the house, in his master's or mistress's presence; nor offer any opinion, unless asked for it; nor even to say "good night," or "good morning," except in reply to that salutation.

Preserve Cut Flowers

A bouquet of freshly-cut flowers may be preserved alive for a long time by placing them in a glass or vase with fresh water, in which a little charcoal has been steeped, or a small piece of camphor dissolved. The vase should be set upon a plate or dish, and covered with a bell-glass, around the edges of which, when it comes in contact with the plate, a little water should be poured to exclude the air. Plunge the stems into boiling water, and by the time the water is cold, the flowers will have revived. Then cut afresh the ends of the stems, and keep them in fresh cold water.

8

Functions of Cleaning Workers

Building cleaning workers-including janitors, maids, housekeeping cleaners, window washers, and rug shampooers-keep office buildings, hospitals, stores, apartment houses, hotels, and residences clean and in good condition. Some only do cleaning, while others have a wide range of duties.

Janitors and cleaners perform a variety of heavy cleaning duties, such as cleaning floors, shampooing rugs, washing walls and glass, and removing rubbish. They may fix leaky faucets, empty trash cans, do painting and carpentry, replenish bathroom supplies, mow lawns, and see that heating and air-conditioning equipment works properly. On a typical day, janitors may wet- or dry-mop floors, clean bathrooms, vacuum carpets, dust furniture, make minor repairs, and exterminate insects and rodents.

They also clean snow or debris from sidewalks in front of buildings and notify management of the need for major repairs. While janitors typically perform most of the duties mentioned, cleaners tend to work for companies that specialize in one type of cleaning activity, such as washing windows. Maids and housekeeping cleaners perform any combination of light cleaning duties to maintain private households or commercial establishments, such as hotels, restaurants, and hospitals, clean and orderly.

In hotels, aside from cleaning and maintaining the premises, maids and housekeeping cleaners may deliver ironing boards, cribs, and rollaway beds to guests' rooms. In hospitals, they also may wash bedframes, brush mattresses, make beds, and disinfect and sterilize equipment and supplies with germicides and sterilizing equipment. Janitors, maids, and cleaners use various equipment, tools, and cleaning materials.

For one job they may need a mop and bucket, for another an electric polishing machine and a special cleaning solution. Improved building materials, chemical cleaners, and power equipment have made many tasks easier and less time consuming, but cleaning workers must learn the proper use of equipment and cleaners to avoid harming floors, fixtures, and themselves.

Cleaning supervisors coordinate, schedule, and supervise the activities of janitors and cleaners. They assign tasks and inspect building areas to see that work has been done properly, issue supplies and equipment, and inventory stocks to ensure that an adequate amount of supplies is present. They also screen and hire job applicants, train new and experienced employees, and recommend promotions, transfers, or dismissals.

Supervisors may prepare reports concerning the occupancy of rooms, hours worked, and department expenses. Some also perform cleaning duties. Cleaners and servants in private households dust and polish furniture; sweep, mop, and wax floors; vacuum; and clean ovens, refrigerators, and bathrooms. They also may wash dishes, polish silver, and change and make beds. Some wash, fold, and iron clothes; a few wash windows. General houseworkers also may take clothes and laundry to the cleaners, buy groceries, and perform many other errands.

WORKING CONDITIONS

Because most office buildings are cleaned while they are empty, many cleaning workers work evening hours. Some, however, such as school and hospital custodians, work in the daytime. When there is a need for 24-hour maintenance, janitors may be assigned to shifts. Most full-time building cleaners work about 40 hours a week. Part-time cleaners usually work in the evenings and on weekends.

Building cleaning workers in large office and residential buildings often work in teams consisting of workers who specialize in vacuuming, picking up trash, and cleaning rest rooms, among other things. Supervisors conduct inspections to ensure that the building is cleaned properly and the team is functioning efficiently. Building cleaning workers usually work inside heated, well-lighted buildings. However, they sometimes work outdoors, sweeping walkways, mowing lawns, or shoveling snow.

Working with machines can be noisy, and some tasks, such as cleaning bathrooms and trash rooms, can be dirty and unpleasant. Janitors may suffer cuts, bruises, and burns from machines, handtools, and chemicals. They spend most of their time on their feet, sometimes lifting or pushing heavy furniture or equipment. Many tasks, such as dusting or sweeping, require constant bending, stooping, and stretching. As a result, janitors also may suffer back injuries and sprains.

EMPLOYMENT

Building cleaning workers held nearly 4 million jobs in 2002. More than 6 percent were self-employed. Janitors and cleaners work in nearly every type of establishment and held about 2.3 million jobs. They accounted for about 57 percent of all building cleaning workers. About 28 percent worked for firms supplying building maintenance services on a contract basis, 21 percent were employed in educational institutions, and 2 percent worked in hotels. Other employers included hospitals, restaurants, religious institutions, manufacturing firms, government agencies, and operators of apartment buildings, office buildings, and other types of real estate.

First-line supervisors of housekeeping and janitorial workers held about 230,000 jobs. Approximately 22 percent worked in firms supplying building maintenance services on a contract basis, 14 percent were employed in hotels, 7 percent held jobs in nursing and other residential care facilities, and 5 percent worked in hospitals. Other employers included educational institutions and amusement and recreation facilities.

Maids and housekeepers held about 1.5 million jobs. Hotels, motels, and other traveler accommodations employed the most maids and housekeepers-27 percent-while private households employed the second most: 25 percent. Eight percent were employed in hospitals; and, a similar percentage worked in nursing and other residential care facilities. Although cleaning jobs can be found in all cities and towns, most are located in highly populated areas where there are many office buildings, schools, apartment houses, nursing homes, and hospitals.

Training, Other Qualifications, and Advancement

No special education is required for most janitorial or cleaning jobs, but beginners should know simple arithmetic and be able to follow instructions. High school shop courses are helpful for jobs involving repair work. Most building cleaners learn their skills on the job. Usually, beginners work with an experienced cleaner, doing routine cleaning. As they gain more experience, they are assigned more complicated tasks.

In some cities, programs run by unions, government agencies, or employers teach janitorial skills. Students learn how to clean buildings thoroughly and efficiently, how to select and safely use various cleansing agents, and how to operate and maintain machines, such as wet and dry vacuums, buffers, and polishers. Students learn to plan their work, to follow safety and health regulations, to interact positively with people in the buildings they clean, and to work without supervision. Instruction in minor electrical, plumbing, and other repairs also may be given.

Those who come in contact with the public should have good communication skills. Employers usually look for dependable, hard-working individuals who are in good health, follow directions well, and get along with other people. Building cleaners usually find work by answering newspaper advertisements, applying directly to organizations where they would like to work, contacting local labor unions, or contacting State employment service offices.

Advancement opportunities for workers usually are limited in organizations where they are the only maintenance worker. Where there is a large maintenance staff, however, cleaning workers can be promoted to supervisor and to area supervisor or manager. A high school diploma improves the chances for advancement. Some janitors set up their own maintenance or cleaning businesses.

Supervisors usually move up through the ranks. In many establishments, they are required to take some inservice training to improve their housekeeping techniques and procedures and to enhance their supervisory skills. A small number of cleaning supervisors and managers are members of the International Executive Housekeepers Association, which offers two kinds of certification programs to cleaning supervisors and managers: Certified Executive Housekeeper (CEH) and Registered Executive Housekeeper (REH).

The CEH designation is offered to those with a high school education, while the REH designation is offered to those who have a 4-year college degree. Both designations are earned by attending courses and passing exams, and both must be renewed every 2 years to ensure that workers keep abreast of new cleaning methods. Those with the REH designation usually oversee the cleaning services of hotels, hospitals, casinos, and other large institutions that rely on well-trained experts for their cleaning needs.

Job Outlook

Overall employment of building cleaning workers is expected to grow about as fast as the average for all occupations through 2012, as more office complexes, apartment houses, schools, factories, hospitals, and other buildings requiring cleaning are built to accommodate a growing population and economy. As many firms reduce costs by contracting out the cleaning and maintenance of buildings, businesses providing janitorial and cleaning services on a contract basis are expected to be one of the faster growing employers of these workers.

Although there have been some improvements in productivity in the way buildings are cleaned and maintained-using teams of cleaners, for example, and better cleaning supplies-it is still very much a labor-intensive job. Average growth is expected among janitors and cleaners and among cleaning supervisors, but less-than-average growth is projected for maids and housekeeping cleaners. In addition to job openings arising due to growth, numerous openings should result from the need to replace those who leave this very large occupation each year.

Limited formal education and training requirements, low pay, and numerous part-time and temporary jobs induce many to leave the occupation, thereby contributing to the number of job openings and the need to replace these workers. Much of the growth in these occupations will come from cleaning residential properties. As families become more pressed for time, they increasingly are hiring cleaning and handyman services to perform a variety of tasks in their homes.

Also, as the population ages, older people will need to hire cleaners to help maintain their houses. In addition, housekeeping cleaners will be needed to clean the growing number of residential care facilities for the elderly. These facilities, including assisted-living arrangements, generally provide housekeeping services as part of the rent.

Earnings

Median annual earnings of janitors and cleaners, except maids and housekeeping cleaners, were $18,250 in 2002. The middle 50 percent earned between $14,920 and $23,650. The lowest 10 percent earned less than $12,920, and the highest 10 percent earned more than $30,700. Median annual earnings in 2002 in the industries employing the largest numbers of janitors and cleaners, except maids and housekeeping cleaners, were as follows:

Elementary and secondary schools	$22,820
Local government	22,770
Colleges, universities, and professional schools	21,540
Lessors of real estate	20,240
Services to buildings and dwellings	16,370

Median annual earnings of maids and housekeepers were $16,440 in 2002. The middle 50 percent earned between

$14,210 and $19,400. The lowest 10 percent earned less than $12,560, and the highest 10 percent earned more than $23,750. Median annual earnings in 2002 in the industries employing the largest numbers of maids and housekeepers were as follows:

General medical and surgical hospitals	$18,050
Community care facilities for the elderly	16,470
Nursing care facilities	16,440
Services to buildings and dwellings	16,210
Traveler accommodation	15,740

Median annual earnings of first-line supervisors and managers of housekeeping and janitorial workers were $28,140 in 2002. The middle 50 percent earned between $21,520 and $36,940. The lowest 10 percent earned less than $17,490, and the highest 10 percent earned more than $46,570. Median annual earnings in 2002 in the industries employing the largest numbers of first-line supervisors and managers of housekeeping and janitorial workers were as follows:

Elementary and secondary schools	$33,080
General medical and surgical hospitals	29,000
Nursing care facilities	26,960
Services to buildings and dwellings	25,410
Traveler accommodation	22,710

Related Occupations

Workers who specialize in one of the many job functions of janitors and cleaners include pest control workers; industrial machinery installation, repair, and maintenance workers; and grounds maintenance workers.

9

Functions of Coachman, Groom and Stable-boy

The horse is the noblest of quadrupeds, whether we view him in his strength, his sagacity, or his beauty. He is also the most useful to man of all the animal creation; but his delicacy is equal to his power and usefulness. No other animal, probably, is so dependent on man in the state of domestication to which he has been reduced, or deteriorates so rapidly under exposure, bad feeding, or bad grooming.

It is, therefore, a point of humanity, not to speak of its obvious impolicy, for the owner of horses to overlook any neglect in their feeding or grooming. His interest dictates that so valuable an animal should be well housed, well fed, and well groomed; and he will do well to acquire so much of stable lore as will enable him to judge of these points himself. In a general way, where a horse's coat is habitually rough and untidy, there is a sad want of elbow-grease in the stable. When a horse of tolerable breeding is dull and spiritless, he is getting ill or badly fed; and where he is observed to perspire much in the stables, is overfed, and probably eats his litter in addition to his regular supply of food.

The architectural form of the stables will be subject to other influences than ours; we confine ourselves, therefore, to their internal arrangements. They should be roomy in proportion to the number of stalls; warm, with good ventilation, and perfectly free from cold draughts; the stalls roomy, without excess, with good and well-trapped drainage, so as to exclude bad smells; a sound ceiling to prevent the entrance of dust from the hayloft, which is usually above them; and there should be plenty of light, coming, however, either from above or behind, so as not to glare in the horse's eye.

The first of these objects is attained, if the stables are kept within a degree or two of 50° in winter, and 60° in summer; although some grooms insist on a much higher temperature, in the interests of their own labour. Ventilation is usually attained by the insertion of one or more tubes or boxes of wood or iron through the ceiling and the roof, with a sloping covering over the opening, to keep out rain, and valves or ventilators below to regulate the atmosphere, with openings in the walls for the admission of fresh air: this is still a difficulty, however; for the effluvium of the stable is difficult to dispel, and draughts must be avoided.

This is sometimes accomplished by means of hollow walls with gratings at the bottom outside, for the exit of bad air, which is carried down through the hollow walls and discharged at the bottom, while, for the admission of fresh air, the reverse takes place: the fresh by this means gets diffused and heated before it is discharged into the stable. The Stalls should be divided by partitions of wood-work eight or nine feet high at the head and six at the heels, and nine feet deep, so as to separate each horse from its neighbour.

A hay-rack placed within easy reach of the horse, of wood or iron, occupies either a corner or the whole breadth of the stall, which should be about six feet for on ordinary-sized horse. A manger, formerly of wood, but of late years more generally of iron lined with enamel, occupies a corner of the stall. The pavement of the stall should be nearly level, with a slight incline towards the gutter, to keep the bed dry, paved with hard Dutch brick laid on edge, or asphalte, or smithy clinkers, or rubble-stones, laid in strong cement. In the centre, about five feet from the wall, a grating should be firmly fixed in the pavement, and in communication with a well-trapped drain to carry off the water; the gutter outside the stall should also communicate with the drains by trapped openings.

The passage between the stall and the hall should be from five to six feet broad at least; on the wall, opposite to each stall, pegs should be placed for receiving the harness and other things in daily use. A Harness-room is indispensable to every stable. It should be dry and airy, and furnished with a fireplace and boiler, both for the protection of the harness and to prepare mashes for the horses when required. The partition-wall should be boarded where the harness goes, with pegs to hang the various pieces of harness on, with saddle-trees to rest the saddles on, a cupboard for the brushes, sponges, and leathers, and a lock-up corn-bin.

The furniture of a stable with coachhouse, consists of coach-mops, jacks for raising the wheels, horse-brushes, spoke-brushes, water-brushes, crest and bit-brushes, dandy-brushes, currycombs, birch and heath brooms, trimming-combs, scissors and pickers, oil-cans and brushes, harness-brushes of three sorts, leathers, sponges for horse and carriage, stable-forks, dung-baskets or wheelbarrow, corn-sieves and measures, horse-cloths and stable pails, horn or glass lanterns. Over the stables there should be accommodation for the coachman or groom to sleep. Accidents sometimes occur, and he should be at hand to interfere.

The Establishment we have in view will consist of coachman, groom, and stable-boy, who are capable of keeping in perfect order four horses, and perhaps the pony. Of this establishment the coachman is chief. Besides skill in driving, he should possess a good general knowledge of horses; he has usually to purchase provender, to see that the horses are regularly fed and properly groomed, watch over their condition, apply simple remedies to trifling ailments in the animals under his charge, and report where he observes symptoms of more serious ones which he does not understand. He has either to clean the carriage himself, or see that the stable-boy does it properly.

The Groom's first duties are to keep his horses in condition; but he is sometimes expected to perform the duties of a valet, to ride out with his master, on occasions, to wait at table, and otherwise assist in the house: in these cases, he should have the means of dressing himself, and keeping his clothes entirely away from the stables. In the morning, about six o'clock, or rather before, the stables should be opened and cleaned out, and the horses fed, first by cleaning the rack and throwing in fresh hay, putting it lightly in the rack, that the horses may get it out easily; a short time afterwards their usual morning feed of oats should be put into the manger.

While this is going on, the stable-boy has been removing the stable-dung, and sweeping and washing out the stables, both of which should be done every day, and every corner carefully swept, in order to keep the stable sweet and clean. The real duties of the groom follow: where the horses are not taken out for early exercise, the work of grooming immediately commences.

"Having tied up the head," to use the excellent description of the process given by old Barrett, "take a currycomb and curry him all over the body, to raise the dust, beginning first at the neck, holding the left cheek of the headstall in the left hand, and curry him from the setting-on of his head all over the body to the buttocks, down to the point of the hock; then change your hands, and curry him before, on his breast, and, laying your right arm over his back, join your right side to his left, and curry him all under the belly near the fore-bowels, and so all over from the knees and back upwards; after that, go to the far side and do that likewise.

Then take a dead horse's tail, or, failing that, a cotton dusting-cloth, and strike that away which the currycomb hath raised. Then take a round brush made of bristles, with a leathern handle, and dress him all over, both head, body, and legs, to the very fetlocks, always cleansing the brush from the dust by rubbing it with the currycomb. In the curry-combing process, as well as brushing, it must be applied with mildness, especially with fine-skinned horses; otherwise the tickling irritates them much.

The brushing is succeeded by a hair-cloth, with which rub him all over again very hard, both to take away loose hairs and lay his coat; then wash your hands in fair water, and rub him all over while they are wet, as well over the head as the body. Lastly, take a clean cloth, and rub him all over again till he be dry; then take another hair-cloth, and rub all his legs exceeding well from the knees and hocks downwards to his hoofs, picking and dressing them very carefully about the fetlocks, so as to remove all gravel and dust which will sometimes lie in the bending of the joints."

In addition to the practice of this old writer, modern grooms add wisping, which usually follows brushing. The best wisp is made from a hayband, untwisted, and again doubled up after being moistened with water: this is applied to every part of the body, as the brushing had been, by changing the hands, taking care in all these operations to carry the hand in the direction of the coat.

Stains on the hair are removed by sponging, or, when the coat is very dirty, by the water-brush; the whole being finished off by a linen or flannel cloth. The horsecloth should now be put on by taking the cloth in both hands, with the outside next you, and, with your right hand to the off side, throw it over his back, placing it no farther back than will leave it straight and level, which will be about a foot from the tail. Put the roller round, and the pad-piece under it, about six or eight inches from the fore legs.

The horse's head is now loosened; he is turned about in his stall to have his head and ears rubbed and brushed over every part, including throat, with the dusting-cloth, finishing by "pulling his ears," which all horses seem to enjoy very much. This done, the mane and foretop should be combed out, passing a wet sponge over them, sponging the mane on both sides, by throwing it back to the midriff, to make it lie smooth.

The horse is now returned to his headstall, his tail combed out, cleaning it of stains with a wet brush or sponge, trimming both tail and mane, and forelock when necessary, smoothing them down with a brush on which a little oil has been dropped. Watering usually follows dressing; but some horses refuse their food until they have drunk: the groom should not, therefore, lay down exclusive rules on this subject, but study the temper and habits of his horse.

All horses not in work require at least two hours' exercise daily; and in exercising them a good groom will put them through the paces to which they have been trained. In the case of saddle-horses he will walk, trot, canter, and gallop them, in order to keep them up to their work. With draught horses they ought to be kept up to a smart walk and trot. Feeding must depend on their work, but they require feeding three times a day, with more or less corn each time, according to their work.

In the fast coaching days it was a saying among proprietors, that "his belly was the measure of his food;" but the horse's appetite is not to be taken as a criterion of the quantity of food under any circumstances. Horses have been known to consume 40 lbs. of hay in twenty-four hours, whereas 16 lbs. to 18 lbs. is the utmost which should have been given. Mr. Croall, an extensive coach proprietor in Scotland, limited his horses to 4-1/2 lbs. cut straw, 8 lbs. bruised oats, and 2-1/2 lbs. bruised beans, in the morning and noon, giving them at night 25 lbs. of the following; viz., 560 lbs. steamed potatoes, 36 lbs. barley-dust, 40 lbs. cut straw, and 6 lbs. salt, mixed up together: under this the horses did their work well.

The ordinary measure given a horse is a peck of oats, about 40 lbs. to the bushel, twice a day, a third feed and a rack-full of hay, which may be about 15 lbs. or 18 lbs., when he is in full work. You cannot take up a paper without having the question put, "Do you bruise your oats?" Well, that depends on circumstances: a fresh young horse can bruise its own oats when it can get them; but aged horses, after a time, lose the power of masticating and bruising them, and bolt them whole; thus much impeding the work of digestion.

For an old horse, then, bruise the oats; for a young one it does no harm and little good. Oats should be bright and dry, and not too new. Where they are new, sprinkle them with salt and water; otherwise, they overload the horse's stomach. Chopped straw mixed with oats, in the proportion of a third of straw or hay, is a good food for horses in full work; and carrots, of which horses are remarkably fond, have a perceptible effect in a short time on the gloss of the coat.

The water given to a horse merits some attention; it should not be too cold; hard water is not to be recommended; stagnant or muddy water is positively injurious; river water is the best for all purposes; and anything is preferable to spring water, which should be exposed to the sun in summer for an hour or two, and stirred up before using it; a handful of oatmeal thrown into the pail will much improve its quality.

A horse should not be sent on a journey or any other hard work immediately after new shoeing;-- the stiffness incidental to new shoes is not unlikely to bring him down. A day's rest, with reasonable exercise, will not be thrown away after this operation. On reaching home very hot, the groom should walk him about for a few minutes; this done, he should take off the moisture with the scraper, and afterwards wisp him over with a handful of straw and a flannel cloth: if the cloth is dipped in some spirit, all the better.

He should wash, pick, and wipe dry the legs and feet, take off the bridle and crupper, and fasten it to the rack, then the girths, and put a wisp of straw under the saddle. When sufficiently cool, the horse should have some hay given him, and then a feed of oats: if he refuse the latter, offer him a little wet bran, or a handful of oatmeal in tepid water. When he has been fed, he should be thoroughly cleaned, and his body-clothes put on, and, if very much harassed with fatigue, a little good ale or wine will be well bestowed on a valuable horse, adding plenty of fresh litter under the belly.

Bridles: Every time a horse is unbridled, the bit should be carefully washed and dried, and the leather wiped, to keep them sweet, as well as the girths and saddle, the latter being carefully dried and beaten with a switch before it is again put on. In washing a horse's feet after a day's work, the master should insist upon the legs and feet being washed thoroughly with a sponge until the water flows over them, and then rubbed with a brush till quite dry.

Harness, if not carefully preserved, very soon gets a shabby tarnished appearance. Where the coachman has a proper harness-room and sufficient assistance, this is inexcusable and easily prevented. The harness-room should have a wooden lining all round, and be perfectly dry and well ventilated. Around the walls, hooks and pegs should be placed, for the several pieces of harness, at such a height as to prevent their touching the ground; and every part of the harness should have its peg or hook,– one for the halters, another for the reins, and others for snaffles and other bits and metal-work; and either a wooden horse or saddle-trees for the saddles and pads. All these parts should be dry, clean, and shining.

This is only to be done by careful cleaning and polishing, and the use of several requisite pastes. The metallic parts, when white, should be cleaned by a soft brush and plate-powder; the copper and brass parts burnished with rottenstone-powder and oil,– steel with emery-powder; both made into a paste with a little oil. An excellent paste for polishing harness and the leather-work of carriages, is made by melting 8 lbs. of yellow wax, stirring it till completely dissolved.

Into this pour 1 lb. of litharge of the shops, which has been pounded up with water, and dried and sifted through a sieve, leaving the two, when mixed, to simmer on the fire, stirring them continually till all is melted. When it is a little cool, mix this with 1-1/4 lb. of good ivory-black; place this again on the fire, and stir till it boils anew, and suffer it to cool. When cooled a little, add distilled turpentine till it has the consistence of a thickish paste, scenting it with any essence at hand, thinning it when necessary from time to time, by adding distilled turpentine.

When the leather is old and greasy, it should be cleaned before applying this polish, with a brush wetted in a weak solution of potass and water, washing afterwards with soft river water, and drying thoroughly. If the leather is not black, one or two coats of black ink may be given before applying the polish. When quite dry, the varnish should be laid on with a soft shoe-brush, using also a soft brush to polish the leather. When the leather is very old, it may be softened with fish-oil, and, after putting on the ink, a sponge charged with distilled turpentine passed over, to scour the surface of the leather, which should be polished as above.

For fawn or yellow-coloured leather, take a quart of skimmed milk, pour into it 1 oz. of sulphuric acid, and, when cold, add to it 4 oz. of hydrochloric acid, shaking the bottle gently until it ceases to emit white vapours; separate the coagulated from the liquid part, by straining through a sieve, and store it away till required. In applying it, clean the leather by a weak solution of oxalic acid, washing it off immediately, and apply the composition when dry with a sponge.

Wheel-grease is usually purchased at the shops; but a good paste is made as follows:-- Melt 80 parts of grease, and stir into it, mixing it thoroughly and smoothly, 20 parts of fine black-lead in powder, and store away in a tin box for use. This grease is used in the mint at Paris, and is highly approved. Carriages in an endless variety of shapes and names are continually making their appearance; but the hackney cab or clarence seems most in request for light carriages; the family carriage of the day being a modified form of the clarence adapted for family use.

The carriage is a valuable piece of furniture, requiring all the care of the most delicate upholstery, with the additional disadvantage of continual exposure to the weather and to the muddy streets. It requires, therefore, to be carefully cleaned before putting away, and a coach-house perfectly dry and well ventilated, for the wood-work swells with moisture; it shrinks also with heat, unless the timber has undergone a long course of seasoning: it should also have a dry floor, a boarded one being recommended.

It must be removed from the ammoniacal influence of the stables, from open drains and cesspools, and other gaseous influences likely to affect the paint and varnish. When the carriage returns home, it should be carefully washed and dried, and that, if possible, before the mud has time to dry on it. This is done by first well slushing it with clean water, so as to wash away all particles of sand, having first closed the sashes to avoid wetting the linings.

The body is then gone carefully over with a soft mop, using plenty of clean water, and penetrating into every corner of the carved work, so that not an atom of dirt remains; the body of the carriage is then raised by placing the jack under the axletree and raising it so that the wheel turns freely; this is now thoroughly washed with the mop until the dirt is removed, using a water-brush for corners where the mop does not penetrate.

Every particle of mud and sand removed by the mop, and afterwards with a wet sponge, the carriage is wiped dry, and, as soon after as possible, the varnish is carefully polished with soft leather, using a little sweet oil for the leather parts, and even for the panels, so as to check any tendency of the varnish to crack. Stains are removed by rubbing them with the leather and sweet oil; if that fails, a little Tripoli powder mixed with the oil will be more successful.

In preparing the carriage for use, the whole body should be rubbed over with a clean leather and carefully polished, the iron-work and joints oiled, the plated and brass-work occasionally cleaned,– the one with plate-powder, or with well-washed whiting mixed with sweet oil, and leather kept for the purpose,– the other with rottenstone mixed with a little oil, and applied without too much rubbing, until the paste is removed; but, if rubbed every day with the leather, little more will be required to keep it untarnished.

The linings require careful brushing every day, the cushions being taken out and beaten, and the glass sashes should always be bright and clean. The wheel-tires and axletree are carefully seen to, and greased when required, the bolts and nuts tightened, and all the parts likely to get out of order overhauled. These duties, however, are only incidental to the coachman's office, which is to drive; and much of the enjoyment of those in the carriage depends on his proficiency in his art,– much also of the wear of the carriage and horses.

He should have sufficient knowledge of the construction of the carriage to know when it is out of order,– to know, also, the pace at which he can go over the road he has under him, without risking the springs, and without shaking those he is driving too much. Having, with or without the help of the groom or stable-boy, put his horses to the carriage, and satisfied himself, by walking round them, that everything is properly arranged, the coachman proceeds to the off-side of the carriage, takes the reins from the back of the horses, where they were thrown, buckles them together, and, placing his foot on the step, ascends to his box, having his horses now entirely under control.

In ordinary circumstances, he is not expected to descend, for where no footman accompanies the carriage, the doors are usually so arranged that even a lady may let herself out, if she wishes it, from the inside. The coachman's duties are to avoid everything approaching an accident, and all his attention is required to guide his horses. The pace at which he drives will depend upon his orders,– in all probability a moderate pace of seven or eight miles an hour; less speed is injurious to the horses, getting them into lazy and sluggish habits; for it is wonderful how soon these are acquired by some horses.

The writer was once employed to purchase a horse for a country friend, and he picked a very handsome gelding out of Collins's stables, which seemed to answer to his friend's wants. It was duly committed to the coachman who was to drive it, after some very successful trials in harness and out of it, and seemed likely to give great satisfaction.

After a time, the friend got tired of his carriage, and gave it up; as the easiest mode of getting rid of the horse, it was sent up to the writer's stables,-- a present. Only twelve months had elapsed; the horse was as handsome as ever, with plenty of flesh, and a sleek glossy coat, and he was thankfully enough received; but, on trial, it was found that a stupid coachman, who was imbued with one of their old maxims, that "it's the pace that kills," had driven the horse, capable of doing his nine miles an hour with ease, at a jog-trot of four miles, or four and a half; and now, no persuasion of the whip could get more out of him.

After many unsuccessful efforts to bring him back to his pace, in one of which a break-down occurred, under the hands of a professional trainer, he was sent to the hammer, and sold for a sum that did not pay for the attempt to break him in. This maxim, therefore, "that it's the pace that kills," is altogether fallacious in the moderate sense in which we are viewing it.

In the old coaching days, indeed, when the Shrewsbury "Wonder" drove into the inn yard while the clock was striking, week after week and mouth after month, with unerring regularity, twenty-seven hours to a hundred and sixty-two miles; when the "Quicksilver" mail was timed to eleven miles an hour between London and Plymouth, with a fine of £5 to the driver if behind time; when the Brighton "Age," "tool'd" and horsed by the late Mr. Stevenson, used to dash round the square as the fifth hour was striking, having stopped at the half-way house while his servant handed a sandwich and a glass of sherry to his passengers,-- then the pace was indeed "killing."

But the truth is, horses that are driven at a jog-trot pace lose that élan with which a good driver can inspire them, and they are left to do their work by mere weight and muscle; therefore, unless he has contrary orders, a good driver will choose a smart pace, but not enough to make his horses perspire: on level roads this should never be seen. In choosing his horses, every master will see that they are properly paired,– that their paces are about equal.

When their habits differ, it is the coachman's duty to discover how he can, with least annoyance to the horses, get that pace out of them. Some horses have been accustomed to be driven on the check, and the curb irritates them; others, with harder mouths, cannot be controlled with the slight leverage this affords; he must, therefore, accommodate the horses as he best can. The reins should always be held so that the horses are "in hand;" but he is a very bad driver who always drives with a tight rein; the pain to the horse is intolerable, and causes him to rear and plunge, and finally break sway, if he can.

He is also a bad driver when the reins are always slack; the horse then feels abandoned to himself; he is neither directed nor supported, and if no accident occurs, it is great good luck. The true coachman's hands are so delicate and gentle, that the mere weight of the reins is felt on the bit, and the directions are indicated by a turn of the wrist rather than by a pull; the horses are guided and encouraged, and only pulled up when they exceed their intended pace, or in the event of a stumble; for there is a strong though gentle hand on the reins.

The Whip, in the hands of a good driver, and with well-bred cattle, is there, more as a precaution than a "tool" for frequent use; if he uses it, it is to encourage, by stroking the flanks; except, indeed, he has to punish some waywardness of temper, and then he does it effectually, taking care, however, that it is done on the flank, where there is no very tender part, never on the crupper. In driving, the coachman should never give way to temper. How often do we see horses stumble from being conducted, or at least "allowed," to go over bad ground by some careless driver, who immediately wreaks that vengeance on the poor horse which might, with much more justice, be applied to his own brutal shoulders. The whip is of course useful, and even necessary, but should be rarely used, except to encourage and excite the horses.

10

Restroom Cleaning

Customers expect managers to keep restrooms clean, and yet the end result year after year is that managers are failing. The technology of restroom cleaning is changing, however, giving managers an opportunity to be environmentally friendly in selecting chemicals to support the evolving technology.

Housekeeping managers who can successfully combine the resources of entities such as the U.S. Environmental Protection Agency (EPA) and Green Seal can develop an arsenal of cleaning chemicals that are environmentally friendly - or "green" - priced right, and perform.

Because of ongoing efforts by equipment manufacturers, the EPA and Green Seal, it is now possible for housekeeping managers to have the best of all worlds - to integrate highly productive equipment with environmentally friendly and cost-effective products to enhance the level of cleanliness in restrooms.

Today's marketplace of custodial equipment affords housekeeping managers many advantages in cleaning restrooms, compared with the days of the traditional mop, bucket and wringer. The traditional method, though still in use, is increasingly falling behind the new technologies.

Some new systems are simple, while others are more complex, but most systems enhance the performance of cleaning chemicals - if, in fact, any chemicals are used at all - and all while enabling managers to minimize complaints by effectively cleaning restrooms.

Restroom Cleaning Kits

Vapour Cleaning

These restroom cleaning systems are becoming increasingly popular. The systems use no chemicals. Instead, they use a tank that superheats the water, and operators spray the resulting steam onto the dirty areas with a special wand that features an applicator to which cleaning towels might be attached. The operator wipes all surfaces with the superheated vapor, changing the cloth as it becomes soiled. The units also have special heads that allow for crevice cleaning.

In addition to using these units for cleaning restrooms, cleaning crews also can use them for cleaning kitchens because the steam easily breaks down the grease. Also, when using the wand and towel attachment, the units might be effective in cleaning dirt off walls.

Manufacturers of some of these systems claim that the units require no chemicals, but housekeeping managers should familiarize themselves with the claims and the infection-control needs of their facility. Also, operators need to be aware that the vapor is hot and that handles of some wands might become hot. As a result, they will need to wear appropriate personal protective equipment.

Several manufacturers now market restroom cleaning kits that might include a cleaning cart, a bucket and a series of extension handles with associated specialized mop heads and attachments. The cart has space for storing cleaning supplies and paper products. Increasingly, crews are replacing old cotton-string mops with microfiber flat mops that are easier to use, lighter and enable aggressive cleaning of the surface.

The restroom cleaning kits give the person cleaning restrooms all of the necessary products they might need on the job site. Some advocates of microfiber cleaning cloths say that the cloths eliminate or mitigate the need for cleaning chemicals. Realistically, crews often can enhance their cleaning efforts in restrooms by applying the appropriate chemicals during the cleaning process.

Powered Cleaning Equipment

Specialized power washers for cleaning restrooms have been available for several years now. Generally, the power washer is cart-mounted for carrying limited cleaning supplies and might come in various sizes. Basically, after the floor has been swept, the unit allows the operator to power-wash the restroom from ceiling to floor and to air dry the room before use.

These units have specialized chemicals, applied through a solution pick-up hose, that afford deep cleaning and drying of surfaces without leaving spots, much like an effective dishwashing agent. More advanced units not only can allow an operator to power spray a room but can also pick up the residue solution after cleaning to minimize the time that a restroom is out of service.

When using these units, operators need use all appropriate safety precautions. For example, crews should not spray chemicals into electrical outlets, and they should make sure that paper goods are adequately protected from solution overspray. When used correctly, these units really do deliver deep cleaning to restrooms.

Manufacturers have provided a new generation of equipment for housekeeping managers to specify to improve the level of restroom cleaning in their facilities. Several can help minimize the use of chemicals.

To complement this cleaning process, Green Seal has developed a "Checklist: Green Seal defines a superior cleaning chemical as "one that lessens its environmental impacts at every stage of its life cycle, including its packaging." Among the items on the checklist are the following:

— Products should be both biodegradable and non-toxic.

— Phosphates concentration should be 5 percent of weight or less, and those without are best.

— Products should work in cold water and be concentrated.

— Avoid products with chlorine bleach or sodium hypochlorite.

— When diluted, concentrations of volatile organic chemicals should not exceed 10 percent of the weight.

— Avoid ingredients that are derived from petroleum.

— Choose surfactants derived from vegetable oil. Avoid those with nonylphenol ethoxylate.

— Use products with a neutral pH.

— Choose products that are packaged in recycled containers.

In addition to this information, the U.S. Environmental Protection Agency (EPA) has developed a Database of Environmental Information for Products and Services. The database provides "useful sources of information on the environmental preferability of products and services.

Housekeeping managers who want to curtail complaints concerning their facilities' restrooms and minimize the impact of cleaning chemicals and processes on the environment have more options than ever today. They can achieve these goals by learning about those options.

Today's environmentally friendly chemicals and equipment are increasingly cost competitive, have increased efficacy, limit damage to the environment and minimize costs to an organization for disposal of chemicals. In more cases than ever, it is a winning combination to clean restrooms with green chemicals and equipment that can solve restroom cleaning complaints and control costs at the same time.

Practices of Infection Control

Housekeeping practices, if performed correctly through educational presentations, will create an area suitable for patient, visitor and healthcare worker to enter and be comfortable within the confines of the environment. The proper maintenance of a health care facility increases the awareness of other employees of the necessity of good sanitary practices. Good housekeeping practices increase moral and public relations. No one wants to work in an area that smells or is dirty.

Sanitation depends upon cleaning thoroughness. There should be procedures in writing to fit each area of the facility such as walls, floors, windows, beds, furniture, draperies, carpets, waste containers, bathrooms, equipment, stairs, elevators, special-care equipment and handling of infectious waste for disposal. Some guideline for infection control are given below:

Patient Rooms

— All horizontal surfaces are cleaned daily or as needed with a registered disinfectant.

— Uncarpeted floors are cleaned daily or as needed with a registered disinfectant.

— Carpeted floors should be vacuumed daily or as needed according to manufacturer's recommendations. Procedures should be spelled out concerning disinfecting carpets that contain blood. The vacuum cleaner should be one that does not add airborne organisms to the environment. Change filters as needed.

— Bathroom is cleaned daily or as needed. Remember that this area of the patient's room may contain high concentrations of body fluids that may neutralize the disinfectant being used.

— Sanitary procedures are performed with common sense in mind.

— Drapes are examined for body fluids or soiling. They do not have to be removed from isolation rooms once the patient has either recovered or been placed in a different locale unless body soils are visible. Drapes have never been implicated in cross contamination of patients.

— Walls are only spot cleaned. There is absolutely no need in washing walls after a patient has been dismissed from a room intended for any type of isolation.

— Normal disinfection procedures are employed in cleaning rooms used for isolation.

— If a patient is in isolation such as airborne, then the appropriate masks should be worn upon entering room.

— Gowns and gloves are used accordingly.

— All patient use items (wheelchairs, etc.) should be disinfected with an EPA registered disinfectant as needed.

— Stainless steel double-bucket system should be used in all areas of the facility. Plastic buckets tend to become soiled and difficult to clean.

— All waste paper baskets should be lined with a plastic bag.

— Housekeeping personnel should report to the executive housekeepers any equipment that is not functioning correctly.

— Make certain that all MSDS forms are up to date.

Other Areas

— Entrances, lobbies, waiting rooms, hallways should be cleaned on a regular schedule or as needed depending on traffic.

— A disinfectant solutions is not really needed in these areas.

— Clean carpets according to manufacturer's recommendations. Make certain that you have discussed with the manufacturer that if blood is spilled on these carpets, what type of chemicals can be used without damaging the fabric. Remember that you must use a tuberculocidal disinfectant on blood spills.

— Examine walls for soilage. Spot clean any wall that contains soil.

Personnel

— Personnel should be free of skin lesions such as herpes, boils, etc.

— All employees in housekeeping should be educated on what requires work restriction due to illness.

— All housekeeping personnel should be ideally vaccinated against tetanus, hepatitis B and influenza. The chickenpox vaccine is now available for those without prior history of exposure or immunity.

— Rubella and measles vaccine should be part of the employee's responsibility prior to employment.

Regulated Trash

— All housekeeping personnel should be cognizant on what types of waste require regulation. OSHA has defined what requires regulation. However, states, city's and county's may have additional requirements. They should be listed in the procedure manual.

— All housekeeping personnel should have inservice education on Standard Precautions (formerly Universal Precautions) on a yearly basis. Documentation of such education should be made available to any licensing agency.

SUMMATION

— Contamination of the environment is only a risk to the patient if there is a potential mode of transmission.

— Housekeeping is responsible for selecting a disinfectant, writing procedures on how to dilute it and when it should be changed during usage.

— Housekeeping personnel need yearly inservices on infection control practices.

— Cleaning in wrong sequences (soiled to clean) may increase the chance of microbial contamination.

— Use of dry-dusting increases aerosols.

— Use of reusable rather than disposable gloves affords the housekeeper more protection.

— Never store mops in a wet condition. This will increase proliferation of organisms. They should be dried after cleaning.

— Always check with other areas of the hospital/nursing home tomake certain that everyone is doing their job correctly, i.e., surgery, nursery, dietary, etc.

— Make certain that housekeepers understand how to pickup sharps from the floor, i.e., needles.

— Housekeepers must be provided the appropriate barrier protection for their tasks, instructions on where they are located, how to take them off and where to place them after removal.

— All filters in rooms should be checked on a regular schedule. When a filter is removed (changed) from a particular area, the date of newly installed filter should be written clearly on its side with a marking pen. This will enable the housekeeper to determine how often these filters should be changed.

— Change curtains as needed.

— Clean blinds as needed.

— It is not necessary to discard toilet paper or paper towels following patient discharge regardless of the sickness unless they are visibly soiled with body fluids.

— Always make certain that paper towel dispensers are full and that soap dispensers are functional.

— Always check needle disposal boxes to make certain that they are not more than 3/4 full.

— Check to make certain that all screens are functioning correctly.

— Check schedules of waste pickup to make certain that excessive accumulation does not exist.

Every hospital/nursing homes must have in place a written procedure on the type of methods that will be employed to protect the highly susceptible patient from aerosols created during construction projects.

11

Environment Friendly Cleanliness

Cleaning and sanitizing is the most important aspect of a sanitation program. Detailed procedures must be developed for all food-product contact surfaces as well as for non-product surfaces such as: non-product portions of equipment, overhead structures, shield, walls, ceilings, lighting devices, refrigeration units, heating, ventilation and air conditioning (HVAC) systems, and anything else which could impact food safety.

Cleaning frequency must be clearly defined for each process line. The type of cleaning required must also be identified. The objective of cleaning and sanitizing food contact surfaces is to remove food (nutrients) which bacteria need to grow, and to kill those bacteria which are present. It is important that the clean, sanitized equipment and surfaces drain dry and are stored dry soas to prevent bacteria growth. Necessary equipment must also be clean and stored in a clean, sanitary manner.

Cleaning/sanitizing procedures must be evaluated for adequacy through evaluation and inspection procedures. Adherence to prescribed written procedures (inspection, swab testing, direct observation of personnel) should be continuously monitored, and records maintained to evaluate long-term compliance.

The correct order of events for cleaning/ sanitizing of food product contact surfaces is:

— Rinse

— Clean

— Rinse

— Sanitize.

Cleaning

Cleaning is the complete removal of food soil using appropriate detergent chemicals under recommended conditions. It is important that personnel involved have a working understanding of the nature of the different types of food soil and the chemistry of its removal.

Methods

Equipment can be categorized with regard to cleaning method as follows:

— *Mechanical Cleaning*: Often referred to as clean- in-place (CIP) . Require no disassembly or partial disassembly.

— *Clean-out-of-Place (COP)*: Can be partially disassembled and cleaned in specialized COP pressure tanks.

— *Manual Cleaning*: Requires total disassembly for cleaning and inspection.

Sanitization

It is important to differentiate and define certain terminology:

— *Sterilize* refers to the statistical destruction and removal of all living organisms.

— *Disinfect* refers to inanimate objects and the destruction of all vegetative cells (not spores).

— *Sanitize* refers to the reduction of microorganisms to levels considered safe from a public health viewpoint.

Appropriate and approved sanitization procedures are processes and, thus, the duration or time as well as the chemical conditions must be described. The official definition of sanitizing for food product contact surfaces is a process which reduces the contamination level by 99.999% (5 logs) in 30 sec.

The official definition for non-product contact surfaces requires a contamination reduction of 99.9% (3 logs). The standard test organisms used are: Staphylococcus aureus and Escherichia coli. General types of sanitization include:

— *Thermal Sanitization* involves the use of hot water or steam for a specified temperature and contact time.

— *Chemical Sanitization* involves the use of an approved chemical sanitizer at a specified concentration and contact time.

Water Chemistry and Quality

Water comprises approximately 95-99% of cleaning and sanitizing solutions. Water functions to:

— carry the detergent or the sanitizer to the surface

— carry soils or contamination from the surface.

The impurities in water can drastically alter the effectiveness of a detergent or a sanitizer. Water hardness is the most important chemical property with a direct effect on cleaning and sanitizing efficiency. Water pH ranges generally from pH 5 to 8.5. This range is of no serious consequence to most detergents and sanitizers. However, highly alkaline or highly acidic water may require additional buffering agents.

Water can also contain significant numbers of microorganisms. Water used for cleaning and sanitizing must be potable and pathogen-free.

Cleaning: Food Soils

Food soil is generally defined as unwanted matter on food-contact surfaces. Soil is visible or invisible. The primary source of soil is from the food product being handled. However, minerals from water residue and residues from cleaning compounds contribute to films left on surfaces. Microbiological biofilms also contribute to the soil buildup on surfaces.

Since soils vary widely in composition, no one detergent is capable of removing all types. Many complex films contain: combinations of food components, surface oil or dust, insoluble cleaner components, and insoluble hard-water salts. These films vary in their solubility properties depending upon such factors as heat effect, age, dryness, time, etc.

It is essential that personnel involved have an understanding of the nature of the soil to be removed before selecting a detergent or cleaning regime. Therule of thumb is that acid cleaners dissolve alkaline soils (minerals) and alkaline cleaners dissolve acid soils and food wastes. Improper use of detergents can actually "set" soils, making them more difficult to remove (e.g., acid cleaners can precipitate protein). Many films and biofilms require more sophisticated cleaners which are amended with oxidizing agents (such as chlorinated detergents) for removal.

Soils may be classified as:

— soluble in water (sugars, some starches, most salts);

— soluble in acid (limestone and most mineral deposits);

— soluble in alkali (protein, fat emulsions);

— soluble in water, alkali, or acid.

The physical condition of the soil deposits also effects its solubility. Freshly precipitated soil in a cool or cold solution is usually more easily dissolved than an old, dried, or baked-on deposit, or a complex film. Food soils are complex in that they contain mixtures of several components.

Fat

Fat usually is present as an emulsion and can generally be rinsed away with hot water above the melting point. More difficult fat and oil residues can be removed with alkaline detergents which have good emulsifying or saponifying ingredients.

Protein

In the food industry, proteins are by far the most difficult soils to remove. In fact, casein (a major milk protein) is used for its adhesive properties in many glues and paints. Food proteins range from more simple proteins, which are easy to remove, to more complex proteins, which are very difficult to remove. Heat-denatured proteins can be extremely difficult.

Generally, a highly alkaline detergent with peptizing or dissolving properties is required to remove protein soils. Wetting agents can also be used to increase the wettability and suspendability of proteins. Protein films require alkaline cleaners which have hypochlorite in addition to wetting agents.

Carbohydrate

Simple sugars are readily soluble in warm water and are

quite easily removed. Starch residues, individually, are also easily removed with mild detergents. Starches associated with proteins or fatscan usually be easily removed by highly alkaline detergents.

Mineral Salt

Mineral salts can be either relatively easy to remove, or be highly troublesome deposits or films. Calcium and magnesium are involved in some of the most difficult mineral films. Under conditions involving heat and alkaline pH, calcium and magnesium can combine with bicarbonates to form highly insoluble complexes. Other difficult deposits contain iron or manganese.

Salt films can also cause corrosion of some surfaces. Difficult salt films require an acid cleaner (especially organic acids which form complexes with these salts) for removal. Sequestering agents such as phosphates or chelating agents are often used in detergents for salt film removal.

Microbiological films

Under certain conditions, microorgranisms (bacteria, yeasts, and molds) can form invisible films (biofilms) on surfaces. Biofilms can be difficult to remove and usually require cleaners as well as sanitizers with strong oxidizing properties.

Lubricating greases and oils

These deposits (insoluble in water, alkali, or acid) can often be melted with hot water or steam, but oftenleave a residue. Surfactants can be used to emulsify the residue to make it suspendable in water and flushable.

Other Insoluble soils

Inert soils such as sand, clay, or fine metal can be removed by surfactant-based detergents. Charred or carbonized material may require organic solvents.

Quantity of Soil

It is important to rinse food-contact surfaces prior to cleaning to remove most of the soluble soil. Heavy deposits require more detergent to remove. Improper cleaning can actually contribute to build-up of soil.

Surface Characteristics

The cleanability of the surface is a primary consideration in evaluating cleaning effectiveness. Included in surface characteristics are:

— *Surface Composition*: Stainless steel is the preferred surface for food equipment and is specified in many industry and regulatory design and construction standards. For example: 3-A Sanitary Standards (equipment standards used for milk and milk products applications) specify 300 series stainless steel or equivalent. Other grades of stainless steel may be appropriate for specific applications (i.e 400 series) such as handling of high fat products, meats, etc. For highly acidic, high salt, or other highly corrosive products, more corrosion resistant materials (i.e. titanium) is often recommended.

Other "soft" metals (aluminum, brass, copper, or mild steel), or nonmetallic surfaces (plastics, or rubber) are also used on food contact surfaces. Surfaces of soft metals and nonmetallic materials are generally less corrosion- resistant and care should be exercised in their cleaning.

Aluminum is readily attacked by acids as well as highly alkaline cleaners which can render the surface non-cleanable. Plastics are subject to stress cracking and clouding from prolonged exposure to corrosive food materials or cleaning agents.

Hard wood (maple or equivalent) or sealed wood surfaces should only be used in limited applications such as cutting boards or cutting tables provided the surface is maintained in good repair. Avoid using porous wood surfaces.

— *Surface Finish*: Equipment design and construction standards also specify finish and smoothness requirements. 3-A standards specify a finish at least as smooth as a No. 4 ground finish for most application. With high-fat products, a less smooth surface is used to allow product release from the surface.

— *Surface Condition*: Misuse or mishandling can result in pitted, cracked, corroded, or roughened surfaces. Such surfaces are more difficult to clean or sanitize, and may no longer be cleanable. Thus, care should be exercised in using corrosive chemicals or corrosive food products.

Environmental Considerations

Detergents can be significant contributors to the waste discharge(effluent). Of primary concern is pH. Many publicly owned treatment works limit effluent pH to the range of 5 to 8.5. So, it is recommended that in applications where highly alkaline cleaners are used, that the effluent be mixed with rinse water (or some other method be used) to reduce the pH. Recycling of caustic soda cleaners is also becoming a common practice in larger operations. Other concerns are phosphates, which are not tolerated in some regions of the U.S., and the overall soil load in the waste stream which contributes to the chemical oxygen demand (COD) and biological oxygen demand (BOD).

Chemistry of Detergents

Detergents and cleaning compounds are usually composed of mixtures of ingredients that interact with soils in several ways:

— Physically active ingredients alter physical characteristics such as solubility or colloidal stability.

— Chemically active ingredients modify soil components to make them more soluble and, thus, easier to remove.

In some detergents, specific enzymes are added to catalytically react with, and degrade, specific food soil components.

Physically active ingredients

The primary physically active ingredients are the surface active compounds termed surfactants. These organic molecules have general structural characteristicwhere a portion of the structure is hydrophilic (water- loving) and a portion is hydrophobic (not reactive with water). Such molecules function in detergents by promoting the physical cleaning actions through: emulsification, penetration, spreading, foaming, and wetting. The classes of surfactants are:

— *Ionic surfactants* which are negatively charged in water solution are termed anionic surfactants. Conversely, positively charged ionic surfactants are termed cationic surfactants. If the charge of the water soluble portion is depended upon the pH of the solution it is termed an amphoteric surfactant. These surfactants behave as cationic surfactants under acid conditions, and as anionic surfactants under alkaline conditions. Ionic surfactants are generally characterized by their high foaming ability.

— *Nonionic surfactants* , which do not dissociate when dissolved in water, have the broadest range of properties depending upon the ratio of hydrophilic/ hydrophobic balance. This balance is also affected by temperature. For example, the foaming properties of nonionic detergents is affected by temperature of solution. As temperature increases, the hydrophobic character and solubility decreases. At the cloud point (minimum solubility), these surfactants generally act as defoamers, while below the cloud point they are varied in their foaming properties.

It is a common practice to blend surfactant ingredients to optimize their properties. However, because of precipitation problems, cationic and anionic surfactants cannot be blended

Chemically active ingredients

Alkaline Builders: *Highly Alkaline Detergents (or heavy-duty detergents)* use caustic soda (sodium hydroxide) or caustic potash (potassium hydroxide). An important property of these highly alkaline detergents is that they saponify fats: forming soap. These cleaners are used in many CIP systems or bottle-washing applications.

Moderately Alkaline Detergents include sodium, potassium, or ammonium salts of phosphates, silicates, or carbonates. Tri-sodium phosphate (TSP) is one of the oldest and most effective. Silicates are most oftenused as a corrosion inhibitor. Because of interaction with calcium and magnesium and film formation, carbonate-based detergents are of only limited use in food processing cleaning regimes.

Acid Builders: *Acid Detergents* include organic and inorganic acids. The most common inorganic acids used include: phosphoric, nitric, sulfamic, sodium acid sulfate, and hydrochloric. Organic acids, such as hydroxyacetic, citric, and gluconic, are also in use. Acid detergents are often used in a two-step sequential cleaning regime with alkaline detergents. Acid detergents are also used for the prevention or removal of stone films (mineral stone, beer stone, or milk stone).

Water Conditioners: Water conditioners are used to prevent the build-up of various mineral deposits (water hardness, etc.). These chemicals are usually sequestering agents or chelating agents. Sequestering agents form soluble complexes with calcium and magnesium. Examples are sodium tripolyphosphate, tetra-potassium pyrophosphate, organo-phosphates, and polyelectrolytes. Chelating agents include sodium gluconate and ethylene diamine tetracetic acid (EDTA).

Oxidizing agents: Oxidizing agents used in detergent application are hypochlorite (also a sanitizer) and--to a lesser extent -- perborate. Chlorinated detergents are most often used to clean protein residues.

Enzyme Ingredients

Enzyme-based detergents, which are amended with enzymes such as amylases and other carbohydrate-degrading enzymes, proteases, and lipases, are finding acceptance in specialized food industry applications.

The primary advantages of enzyme detergents are that they are more environmentally friendly and often require less energy input (less hot water in cleaning). Uses of most enzyme cleaners are usually limited to unheated surfaces (e.g., cold-milk surfaces). However, new generation enzyme cleaners (currently under evaluation) are expected to have broader application.

Fillers

Fillers add bulk or mass, or dilute dangerous detergent formulations which are difficult to handle. Strong alkalis are often diluted with fillers for ease and safety of handling. Water is used in liquid formulations as a filler. Sodium chloride or sodium sulfate are often fillers in powdered detergent formuations.

Miscellaneous Ingredients

Additional ingredients added to detergents may include: corrosion inhibitors, glycol ethers, and butylcellosolve (improve oil, grease, and carbon r.moval).

SANITIZING

Thermal Sanitizing

As with any heat treatment, the effectiveness of thermal sanitizing is dependant upon a number of factors including: initial contamination load, humidity, pH, temperature, and time.

Steam

The use of steam as a sanitizing process has limited application. It is generally expensive compared to alternatives, and it is difficult to regulate and monitor contact temperature and time. Further, the byproducts of steam condensation can complicate cleaning operations.

Hot Water Sanitizing

Hot-water sanitizing--through immersion (small parts, knives, etc.), spray (dishwashers), or circulating systems--is commonly used. The time required is determined by the temperature of the water. Typical regulatory requirements (Food Code 1995) for use of hot water in dishwashing and utensil sanitizing applications specify: immersion for at least 30 sec. at 77°C (170°F) for manual operations; a final rinse temperature of 74°C (165°F) in single tank, single temperature machines and 82°C (180°F) for other machines.

Many state regulations require a utensil surface temperature of 71°C (160°F) as measured by an irreversibly registering temperature indicator in warewashing machines. Recommendations andrequirements for hot-water sanitizing in food processing may vary. The Grade A Pasteurized Milk Ordinance specifies a minimum of 77°C (170°F) for 5 min. Other recommendations for processing operations are: 85°C (185°F) for 15 min., or 80°C (176°F) for 20 min.

The primary advantages of hot-water sanitization are: relatively inexpensive, easy tc apply and readily available, generally effective over a broad range of microorganisms, relatively non-corrosive, and penetratesinto cracks and crevices. Hot-water sanitization is a slow process which requires come-up and cool-down time; can have high energy costs; and has certain safety concerns for employees. The process also has the disadvantages of forming or contributing to film formations, and shortening the life of certain equipment or parts thereof (gaskets, etc.).

Chemical Sanitizing

The ideal chemical sanitizer should:

— be approved for food contact surface application

— have a wide range or scope of activity.

— destroy microorganisms rapidly.

— be stable under all types of conditions.

— be tolerant of a broad range of environmental conditions.

— be readily solubilized and possess some detergency.

— be low in toxicity and corrosivity.

— be inexpensive.

No available sanitizer meets all of the above criteria. Therefore, it is important to evaluate the properties, advantages, and disadvantages of available sanitizer for each specific application.

Regulatory considerations

The regulatory concerns involved with chemical sanitizers are: antimicrobial activity or efficacy, safety of residues on food contact surfaces, and environmental safety. It is important to follow regulations that apply for each chemical usage situation. The registration of chemical sanitizers and antimicrobial agents for use on food and food product contact surfaces, and on nonproduct contact surfaces, is through the U.S. Environmental Protection Agency (EPA). (Prior to approval and registration, the EPAreviews efficacy and safety data, and product labeling information.

The U.S. Food and Drug Administration (FDA) is primarily involved in evaluating residues form sanitizer use which may enter the food supply. Thus, any antimicrobial agent and its maximum usage level for direct use on food or on food product contact surfaces must be approved by the FDA. Approved no-rinse food contact sanitizes and nonproduct contact sanitzers, their formulations and usage levels are listed in the Code of Federal Regulations.

The U.S. Department of Agriculture (USDA) also maintains lists of antimicrobial compounds (i.e., USDA List of Proprietary Substances and Non Food Product Contact Compounds) which are primarily used in the regulation of meats, poultry, and related products by USDA's Food Safety and Inspection Service (FSIS.).

Sanitizer Effectiveness

Physical factors

Surface Characteristics: Prior to the sanitization process, all surfaces must be clean and thoroughly rinsed to remove any detergent residue. An unclean surface cannot be sanitized. Since the effectiveness of sanitization requires direct contact with the microorganisms, the surface should be free of cracks, pits, or crevices which can harbor microorganisms. Surfaces which contain biofilms cannot be effectively sanitized.

Exposure Time: Generally, the longer time a sanitizer chemical is in contact with the equipment surface, the more effective the sanitization effect; intimate contact is as important as prolonged contact..

Temperature: Temperature is also positively related to microbial kill by a chemical sanitizer. Avoid high temperatures (above 55°C [131°F]) because of the corrosive nature of most chemical sanitizers.

Concentration: Generally, the activity of a sanitizer increases with increased concentration. However, a leveling off occurs at high concentrations. A common misconception regarding chemicals is that "if a little is good, more is better". Using sanitizer concentrations above recommendations does not sanitizer better and, in fact, can be corrosive to equipment and in the long run lead to less cleanability. Follow manufacturer's label instructions.

Soil: The presence of organic matter dramatically reduces the activity of sanitizers and may, in fact, totally inactivate them. The adage is "you cannot sanitize an unclean surface".

Chemical factors

pH: Sanitizers are dramatically affected by the pH of the solution. Many chlorine sanitizers, for example, are almost ineffective at pH values above 7.5.

Water properties: Certain sanitizers are markedly affected by impurities in the water.

Inactivators: Organic and/or inorganic inactivators may react chemically with sanitizers giving rise to non-germicidal products. Some of these inactivators are present in detergent residue. Thus, it is important that surfaces be rinsed prior to sanitization.

Biological factors

The microbiological load can affect sanitizer activity. Also, the type of microorganism present is important. Spores are more resistant than vegetative cells. Certain sanitizers are more active against gram positive than gram negative microorganisms, and vice versa. Sanitizers also vary in their effectiveness against yeasts, molds, fungi, and viruses.

Types of Chemical Sanitizers

The chemicals described here are those approved by FDA for use as no-rinse, food-contact surface sanitizers. In food-handling operations, these are used as rinses, sprayed onto surfaces, or circulated through equipment in CIP operations. In certain applications the chemicals are foamed on a surface or fogged into the air to reduce airborne contamination.

Chlorine-based sanitizers

Chlorine Compounds: Chlorine, in its various forms, is the most commonly used sanitizer in food processing and handling applications. Commonly used chlorine compounds include: liquid chlorine, hypochlorites, inorganic chloramines, and organic chloramines. Chlorine-based sanitizers form hypochlorous acid (HOCl, the most active form) in solution. Available chlorine (the amount of HOCl present) is a function of pH. At pH 5, nearly all is in the form of HOCl. At pH 7.0, approximately 75% is HOCl.

The maximumallowable level for no-rinse applications is 200ppm available chlorine, but recommended usage levels vary. For hypochlorites, an exposure time of 1 min at a minimum concentration of 50ppm and a temperature of 24°C (75°F) is recommended. For each 10°C (18°F) drop in temperature, a doubling of exposure time is recommended. For chloramines, 200ppm for 1 min is recommended.

Chlorine compounds are broad spectrum germicides which act on microbial membranes, inhibit cellular enzymes involved in glucose metabolism, have a lethal effect on DNA, and oxidize cellular protein. Chlorine has activity at low temperature, is relatively cheap, and leaves minimal residue or film on surfaces. The activity of chlorine is dramatically affected by such factors as pH, temperature, and organic load. However, chlorine is less affected by water hardness when compared to other sanitizers.

The major disadvantage to chlorine compound is corrosiveness to many metal surfaces. Health and safety concerns can occur due to skin irritation and mucous membrane damage in confined areas. At low pH (below 4.0), deadly Cl_2 (mustard gas) can form. In recent years, concerns have also been raised about the use of chlorine as a drinking water disinfectant and as an antimicrobial with direct food contact (meat, poultry and shellfish).

This concern is based upon the involvement of chlorine in the formation of potentially carcinogenic trihalomethanes (THMs) under appropriate conditions. While chlorine's benefits as a sanitizer far outweigh these risks, it is under scrutiny.

Chlorine dioxide: Chlorine dioxide (ClO_2) is currently being considered as a replacement for chlorine, since it appears to be more environmentally friendly. Stabilized ClO_2 has FDA approval for most applications in sanitizing equipment or for use as a foam for environmental and non-food contact surfaces. Approval has also been granted for use in flume waters in fruits and vegetable operations and in poultry process waters.

ClO_2 has 2.5 times the oxidizing power of chlorine and, thus, less chemical is required. Typical use concentrations range from 1to 10ppm. ClO_2's primary disadvantages are worker safety and toxicity. Its highly concentrated gases can be explosive and exposure risks to workers is higher thanthat for chlorine. Its rapid decomposition in the presence of light, or at temperatures greater than 50°C (122°F) makes on-site generation a recommended practice.

Iodine

Use of iodine as an antimicrobial agents dates back to the 1800s. This sanitizer exists in many forms and usually exists with a surfactant as a carrier. These mixtures are termed iodophors. The most active agent is the dissociated free iodine. This form is most prevalent at low pH. The amount of dissociation from the surfactant is dependent upon the type of surfactant. Iodine solubility is very limited in water. Generally recommended usage for iodophors is 12.5 to 25ppm for 1 min.

It is generally thought that the bactericidal activity of iodine is through direct halogenation of proteins. More recent theories have centered upon cell wall damage and destruction of microbial enzyme activity. Iodophors, like chlorine compounds, have a very broad spectrum: being active against bacteria, viruses, yeasts, molds, fungi, and protozoans. Iodine is highly temperature-dependent and vaporizes at 120°F. Thus, it is limited to lower temperature applications.

The degree to which iodophors are affected by environmental factors is highly dependant upon properties of the surfactant used in the formulation. Iodophors are generally less affected by organic matter and water hardness than chlorine. However, loss of activity is pronounced at high pH. Iodine has a long history of use in wound treatment. However, ingestion of iodine gas does pose a toxicity risk in closed environments. The primary disadvantage is that iodine can cause staining on some surfaces (especially plastics).

Quaternary Ammonium Compounds (QACs)

Quaternary ammonium compounds (QACs) are a class of compounds which have the general structure as follows (Figure 1):

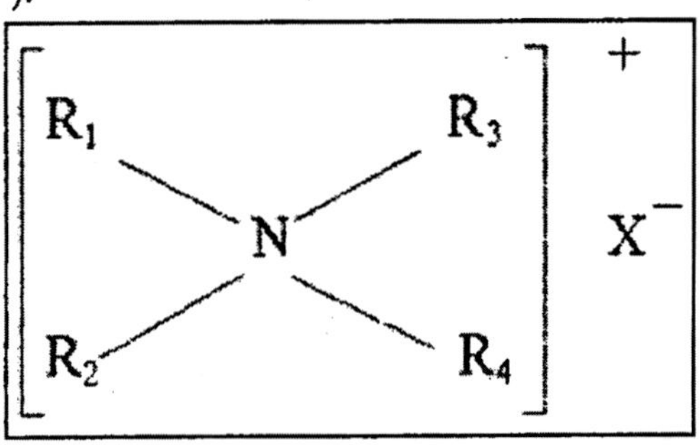

Figure 1. Quaternary Ammonium Compounds (QACs)

The properties of these compounds depend upon the covalently bound alkyl groups (R groups), which can be highly diverse. Since QACs are positively charged cations, their mode of action is related to their attraction to negatively charged materials such as bacterial proteins. It is generally accepted that the mode of action is at the membrane function. The carbon length of R-group side chain is, generally, directly related with sanitizer activity in QACs. However, because of the lower solubility in QACs composed of large carbon chains, these sanitizers may have lower activity than short chain structures.

QACs are active and stable over a broad temperature range. Because they are surfactants, they possess some detergency. Thus, they are less affected by light soil than are other sanitizers. However, heavy soil dramatically decreases activity. QACs generally have higher activity at alkaline pH. While lack of tolerance to hard water is often listed as a major disadvantage of QACs when compared to chlorine, some QACs are fairly tolerant of hard water. Activity can be improved by the use of EDTA as a chelator. QACs are effective against bacteria, yeasts, mold, and viruses.

An advantage of QACs in some applications is that they leave a residual antimicrobial film. However, this would be a disadvantage in operations such as cultured dairy products, cheese, beer, etc. where microbial starter cultures are used. QACs are generally more active against gram positive than gram negative bacteria. They are not highly effective against bacteriophages. Their incompatibility with certain detergents makes thorough rinsing following cleaning operations imperative.Further, many QAC formulations can cause foaming problems in CIP applications.

Under recommended usage and precautions, QACs pose little toxicity or safety risks. Thus, they are in common use as environmental fogs and as room deodorizers. However, care should be exercised in handling concentrated solutions or use as environmental fogging agents.

Acid-Anionic Sanitizers: Like QACs, acid-anionic sanitizers are surface- active sanitizers. These formulations include an inorganic acid plus a surfactant, and are often used for the dual function of acid rinse and sanitization. Whereas QACs are positively charged, these sanitizers are negatively charged. Their activity is moderately affected by water hardness. Their low use pH, detergency, stability, low odor potential, and non-corrosiveness makes them highly desirable in some applications.

Disadvantages include: Relatively high cost, a closely defined pH range of activity (pH 2 to 3), low activity on molds and yeasts, excessive foaming in CIP systems, and incompatibility with cationic surfactant detergents.

Fatty Acid Sanitizers: Fatty acid or carboxylic acid sanitizers were developed in the 1980s. Typical formulations include fatty acids plus other acids (phosphoric acids, organic acids). These agents also have the dual function of acid rinse and sanitization. The major advantage over acid anionics is lower foaming potential. These sanitizers have a broad range of activity, are highly stable in dilute form, are stable to organic matter, and are stable to high temperature applications.

These sanitizers have low activity above pH 3.5 - 4.0, are not very effective against yeasts and molds, and some formulations lose activity at temperatures below 10°C (50°F). They also can be corrosive to soft metals and can degrade certain plastics, or rubber.

Peroxides: Peroxides or peroxy compounds contain at least one pair of covalently bonded oxygen atoms (-O-O-)and are divided into two groups: the inorganic group, containing hydrogen peroxide (HP) and related compounds; and the organic group, containing peroxyacetic acid (PAA) and related compounds.

Hydrogen peroxide (HP): While widely used in the medical field, has found only limited application in the food industry. FDA approval has been granted for HP use for sterilizing equipment and packages in aseptic operations.

The primary mode of action for HP is through creating an oxidizing environment and generation of singlet or superoxide oxygen (SO). HP is fairly broad spectrum with slightly higher activity against gram-negative than gram-positive organisms.

High concentrations of HP (5% and above) can be an eye and skin irritant. Thus, high concentrations should be handled with care. Peroxyacetic Acid (PAA) has been known for its germicidal properties for a long time. However, it has only found food-industry application in recent years and is being promoted as a potential chlorine replacement. PAA is relatively stable at use strengths of 100 to 200ppm. Other desirable properties include: absence of foam and phosphates, low corrosiveness, tolerance to hard water, and favorable biodegradability. PAA solutions have been shown to be useful in removing biofilms.

While precise mode of action mechanisms have not been determined, it is generally theorized that the PAA reaction with microorganisms is similar to that of HP. PAA, however, is highly active against both gram- positive and gram-negative microorganisms. The germicidal activity of PAA is dramatically affected by pH. Any pH increase above 7-8 drastically reduces the activity. PAA has a pungent odor and the concentrated product (40%) is a highly toxic, potent irritant, and powerful oxidizer. Thus, care must be used in its use.

12

Effective Sanitation Programmes

Proper sanitation is important, not only from the standpoint of protecting human health and providing food that is unadulterated with filth or foreign matter, but also from the standpoint of good manufacturing practice, in that proper sanitation will result in an improved keeping capacity for meat products, fewer customer complaints and a generally more acceptable product in the market place.

Sanitation may be defined, in relation to meat hygiene, as the control of environmental influences which may adversely affect the appearance, flavour, shelf life, safety and aesthetic acceptability of meat products. Control in the above context is the judicious exercise of restraining or directing mechanisms that prevent the exposure of meat products to an environment which is hostile to the integrity of the product.

Although when discussing sanitation, the emphasis is placed on the environment, the products themselves must not be over-looked. Dirty or spoiled meat products entering a sanitary environment are not only unacceptable in themselves, but place the environment at risk as well.

— *Hygiene, conditions or practices conducive to health*: as related to cleanliness.

— *Clean*: free from dirt, contamination and disease Contaminate - to make unfit for intended use by the introduction of unwholesome or undesirable elements.

— *Sterilization*: the complete elimination of microbial viability by approved means.

— *Sanitizing*: the process of reducing the level of microorganisms present to a level deemed safe by the regulatory authority.

Facilities and Equipment

These are the fundamental or basic units upon which management builds or creates an atmosphere conducive to the production of safe and aesthetically acceptable meat products. An excellent sanitation program begins with facilities and equipment that are found acceptable as to construction, maintenance and performance. The maintenance of satisfactory sanitary standards depends upon a regular program of cleaning, washing and where necessary, sanitizing, to preclude and remove unwanted contaminants such as bacteria, flaking paint, rust, dust, etc.

It is not the purpose of this manual to illustrate how to clean and sanitize each facility and each piece of equipment. This is the responsibility of management, and the inspection responsibility consists of confirming that the management has effectively performed its role. Sanitation personnel must be familiar with the breakdown and daily cleansing of equipment, utilized within a particular establishment. Inspection personnel should also familiarize themselves with critical areas, critical equipment and critical areas within the equipment.

Housekeeping practices form an integral part of a sanitation program. This will include such actions as garbage collection and disposal, janitorial service during operations, storage and maintenance of equipment temporarily not in use, removal from production areas and storage of obsolete equipment, etc. Poor housekeeping practices may and do encourage the harbouring of bacteria, mould, yeasts androdents and thus negate cleaning and sanitizing of equipment. Contamination can be transferred through contact with employees, trucks, equipment and in the ambient air. A high standard of housekeeping leads to and is an adjunct of an excellent sanitation program.

Chlorination of Water

— Where automatic chlorinators are used in a registered establishment, it is essential that management establish procedures to ensure water potability. Two controls which are fundamental, are as follows:

  — A metering device for adding chlorine in the correct concentration, relative to the waterflow rate, designed to readily indicate malfunction.

  — At least twice daily, tests shall be made to determine the total available chlorine level at a specific point, remotely located from the chlorine application site, but before distribution to the system. An automatic analyzer, equipped with a recorder and alarm system may be utilized as an alternative to the above testing.

  — Hyper-chlorination in poultry plants

  — Hyper-chlorination in red meat plants

Potability of Water and Ice

Analyses may be performed at provincial or municipal public health laboratories or at private laboratories. Private laboratories, including laboratories at registered establishments, can only be used if they have obtained recognition from the provincial authorities having relevant jurisdiction (where that service is provided). If such a recognition service is not provided, the first two options are to be used.

— Frequency and type of analysis

— Bacteriological analysis:

Water: Establishments using only municipal water, require bacteriological analyses on a semi-annual basis with satisfactory results. Establishments supplementing municipal supplies with water from private wells or using solely water from private wells, require bacteriological analyses on a monthly basis with satisfactory results. Whenever a sample is submitted for bacteriological analyses, enumeration of coliforms per 100 ml and total plate count shall be requested.

Ice: Establishments manufacturing ice on site require bacteriological analyses of this ice on a semi-annual basis with satisfactory results or more often as needed. The ice sample shall be taken from the site most likely to cause contamination. Enumeration of coliforms per 100 ml and total plate count shall be requested. Bacterial specifications for ice are as for water. If the testing indicates ice made at the plant is out of compliance all of this ice is held, disposed of and a different source of ice is sought. It is important to identify the cause of the contamination.

The water supply to the ice machine shall be tested immediately and if in compliance with the bacterial specifications a clean-up and sanitation of all the ice equipment is required (ice room, chutes, ice machine etc.). Following this clean-up, the newly made ice shall be tested and must comply with the specifications before the ice can be used.

Establishments purchasing ice from an outside supplier must test the ice for enumeration of coliforms per 100 ml and total plate count (or have the supplier provide a certificate of potability which includes the bacterial results) whenever there is a change in the supplier company, and a minimum two times a year if the ice is from a municipal water source or monthly if the ice is made from other than a municipal water source (eg: well water).

If bacterial testing of the supplied ice indicates that bacterial specifications are not met, the ice must be held and disposed of. The supplier is notified and the next 3 lots from this same supplier must be tested or come with a certificate of potability which includes the bacterial results.

— *Chemical analysis*: Water obtained from municipal supplies need not be sampled at establishments since chemical analysis is carried out at the source. Water from private wells shall be subject to at least one initial chemical analysis with a satisfactory result. The need for any further sampling will be determined by the Chief, Program Development and Evaluation - Chemical Residues, after consultation with provincial health authorities.

— *Requirements of foreign countries*: Establishments approved for export to countries with special requirements must continue to comply with those requirements. e.g. United Kingdom

Water Sample Collection

Management is responsible for the collection and shipment of samples in a satisfactory manner. The site of collection should be varied from sample to sample to provide a maximum coverage of water outlets within the registered establishment. Sterile containers for the collection of samples and instructions regarding shipment should be supplied by laboratories performing the analyses.

Samples for bacterio-logical and chemical analysis shall be collected in appropriate containers. Chlorinated water for bacteriological analysis must be collected in containers with a neutralizing agent, normally 10% sodium thiosulphate solution used at the rate of 2 ml per litre of water. When samples for chemical analysis are being submitted, they should preferably be collected at the end of the spring runoff or immediately following an extended period of wet weather.

Acceptable Methodology

Analysis may be performed at provincial or municipal public health laboratories or in provincially recognized private laboratories.

Minimum acceptable bacteriological standards

Coliform count

The objective level is no coliforms per 100 ml of water. However, water may be adjudged bacteriologically acceptable provided the following tolerances are not exceeded:

- no sample contains more than 10 total coliforms per 100 ml of water;
- not more than 10% of the samples taken in a 30 day period show the presence of coliform organisms;
- not more than 2 consecutive samples from the same site show the presence of coliform organisms; and
- none of the coliform organisms detected are faecal coliforms.

If any coliform organisms were detected, another sample shall be taken from the same site. If the presence of coliforms is confirmed, action shall be taken to determine the cause.

Total bacterial count

The objective level is less than 500 organisms per ml. The result should be used as an indicator for quality control in comparison with other test results on record. A sudden rise over previous levels should be followed up by additional sampling and by an investigation to identify the source of the problem.

In addition, excessive concentration of the general bacterial population can hinder the recovery of coliforms and thereby prevent the detection of a potential threat to public health. Most laboratories do not automatically test for total counts, but will provide this service if requested. Total counts provide a valuable aid in assessing water quality, and shall therefore be requested.

Chemical Standards

The range of chemical analyses will depend on local conditions, such as geological formation, seepage from soil treated with fertilizers, pesticides or local exposure to industrial pollution. To establish the range of tests or repeats required, local Public Health authorities and municipal water plants should be consulted by the Director, Food Inspection.

Physical Characteristics

Potable water should be clear, without offensive taste and odour.

Reporting of test results: Test results should be reported giving bacterial and chemical levels found. In addition, the laboratory should provide a statement to the effect that the water is adjudged to be potable or non-potable, on a bacteriological/chemical basis.

If there is any doubt regarding this assessment, the inspector should contact his regional office for advice. A report of coliform organisms, even if less than 10/100 ml, shall initiate an immediate resampling. Inspectors should review the results with management. Certificates for water potability must be retained by management of the registered establishment for 3 years and be available to the inspection staff.

When a test result indicates limits are exceeded, follow-up sampling shall be initiated immediately by management, consisting of one or more samples taken on three (3) consecutive days. If all samples taken on three consecutive days are negative, weekly sampling for a period of three (3) weeks is to be continued. Two positive test results during followup sampling in the 4 week period make it necessary that remedial action be taken. This may consist of; switching to a noncontaminated source, trucking in potable water, or chlorination or other chemical treatment as indicated.

Steam which may come in contact with product or with product contact areas shall be generated from potable water. The steam supply must be able to meet operational requirements. The manufacturer shall have records to demonstrate the microbiological and chemical safety of the water used to produce the steam supply. Boiler treatment agents must be approved, used according to the manufacturers directions and do not lead to product contamination.

Sanitation Program

The manufacturer has a written cleaning and sanitation program for the entire premises. This program must include all pre-operational and operational procedures and be dated and signed by an official having authority. The operator of a registered establishment shall develop, implement and maintain a sanitation program for all equipment and facilities. In cases where the operator cannot comply with the minimum requirement of washing equipment and facilities with soap and water on a daily basis, he shall make an application to the Chief, Meat Processing Inspection Programs.

The application shall have annexed thereto :

- justification for not doing a daily wash
- a copy of the sanitation program
- the scientific data proving the effectiveness and the safety of the proposed sanitation program compared, where applicable, to the results obtained when doing a daily wash of equipment and installations.

When satisfied that the sanitation program for which an application has been made is effective and safe, the Chief, Meat Processing Inspection Programs could authorize its use.

Written Sanitation Program

The sanitation program shall be kept in written form, signed and dated by the individual with overall authority on-site or an official of the registered establishment.

The sanitation program shall contain:

- the name of the person(s) responsible for carrying out the program,
- the measures taken to ensure that the building, equipment, utensils and all other physical facilities of the registered establishment are maintained in a sanitary condition before and during the operations,
- the frequency of the cleaning and sanitizing activities,
- the equipment and chemical agents use to bring about and maintain clean and sanitary conditions,

— the concentration, temperature and other specifications for the detergent, sanitizer or other chemical agent used, and

— the monitoring activities put in place by the operator to ensure the effectiveness of the sanitation program, including procedures conducted before the start of operations.

The written sanitation program must provide sufficient guidance to ensure that staff responsible for sanitation activities are aware of their responsibilities and have the tools and techniques required to perform sanitation activities in a satisfactory manner. The sanitation program document must be kept up-to-date in order to reflect current activities.

Responsibilities for sanitation activities and the resources allocated for these activities are to be set out in the written program. Hotel management should appoint designated employee(s) to be responsible for sanitation. The sanitation program shall incorporate cleaning schedules and methods that will assure an adequate level of performance. The program specifies the following: areas to be cleaned, method of cleaning to achieve the required efficiency (chemical concentration, application procedures and equipment, contact time, etc.), person responsible, frequency of activity.

It addresses food contact surfaces and equipment, specialized cleaning equipment for a particular equipment (e.g., injectors, grinders, cleaning-in-place, vehicles,...), floors, drains, walls, ceilings, lighting fixtures, refrigeration units, overheads and anything else impacting on food safety. This scheduled sanitation program can be developed in parallel with the preventative maintenance activities for equipment, overheads and other items requiring routine refurbishing and other like attention.

It must be understood that the inspector's responsibility is limited to verifying that the sanitation program is delivered in a manner consistent with the operator's written program and that the program is effective in achieving meat hygiene program objectives with regard to sanitation.

Monitoring of the effectiveness of the sanitation program is the responsibility of lodging management. In addition to pre-operational inspection, checks for effectiveness of the sanitation program shall be instituted. Work procedures, chemical preparation and application procedures and other sanitation activities shall be verified by a hotel management representative on some basis to assure themselves that the written program is being followed.

Microbiological methods as a verification of the effectiveness of the sanitation program should be used, e.g., swab tests contact plates, ATPase tests, Total Plate Count, etc., at a frequency necessary to demonstrate adequacy. The operator of a registered establishment shall retain, for not less than one year after the date of the activity or procedure, written or electronic records that include information on

— the monitoring activities and pre-operational procedures, including the results of any test, and

— any corrective action taken.

Preoperational Inspection

Preoperational inspection of the hotel shall be conducted by a responsible employee to ensure that operations only begin after sanitation requirements have been met. The written program must explain how the preoperational program works, e.g., authority of responsible employee doing the preoperational inspection, responsibilities for ordering corrective action, responsibility for verifying corrective actions, use of reporting forms.

Pre-operational inspection activities must be documented and these documents must be available to the inspector upon request. When deficiencies are identified during the preoperational inspection, they must be noted and acted upon. The corrective action taken shall be indicated on the daily preoperational inspection report, and if immediate correction is required, the corrected item will be verified before use and this verification entered into the report.

The inspector-in-charge's responsibility is to verify that the managements documented program is executed as described and that operations are conducted in a sanitary environment. It is not the inspector's role to conduct regular preoperational inspection for the operator.

Employee training program

Employees must understand the risks associated with contamination of food by microbiological or chemical agents. Employees must be shown the ways to avoid the contamination of the product and they shall be given the proper equipment to achieve this goal.

Training activities must be described in a written employee training program. Employee training must be appropriate for the complexity of the manufacturing process and the tasks assigned. All food handlers must be given appropriate training in personal hygiene and hygienic handling of food at the beginning of their employment.

Additionally, all personnel involved in HACCP systems must be appropriately trained to understand the importance of any critical control point (CCP) for which they are responsible, the critical limits, the procedures for monitoring, the actions to be taken if the limits are not met and the records which are to be kept. Task specific training shall also be outlined in the training document.

Sanitation employees and supervisors must be appropriately trained to understand the principles and methods required for effective cleaning and sanitizing. Shipping and receiving staff must be trained in proper carrier inspection and product handling procedures. Maintenance staff must be appropriately trained in hygienic practices and to identify deficiencies that could affect product safety and to take appropriate corrective action.

Employees responsible for monitoring and calibration activities are also to be trained in proper procedures. Additional training is to be provided whenever changes in equipment or processes dictate updating of procedures. General updates and reinforcements of training at appropriate intervals shall also be included in the training program.

Records

To demonstrate that the written preoperational and operational sanitation, inspection and training programs are being delivered according to the written plans, the operator shall maintain written records of these activities. The records shall demonstrate the effective monitoring and control of these activities. Whenever a deficiency has been identified, it should be noted along with the corrective action taken to resolve the problem. Sanitation records shall be kept on-site for at least one year and be available to the inspector on request.

Responsibility of Inspector

Inspectors are responsible for reviewing and approving the sanitation program developed by management. They are further responsible to monitor the implementation of the sanitation program carried out by management.The implementation of control programs by the inspector will be greatly improved if a spirit of cooperation can be developed with a management which recognizes the benefits that accrue from an adequate sanitation program.

Action must be initiated by the inspector where hotel and equipment sanitation is found unsatisfactory. The type of action may vary from a simple request for rectification of a deficiency to suspension of operations in a room or even an entire establishment. The action must be based on the magnitude of the problem and the associated risk to the integrity of product.

Control Mechanisms

Control mechanisms must be implemented whenever there is a justifiable and identified need. However, they should be applied in a uniform and consistent manner. It is not possible to describe or delineate all the control mechanisms or procedures that may be utilized in the monitoring of a sanitation program.

Those we implement have been developed through a practical application of check systems that assure an environment suitable to the production, handling and processing of a wholesome meat product. The frequency and severity of application have a direct relation to the degree of risk involved, the past history of compliance and possible changes or variations in operating procedures.

Control should not be limited to those systems that have been historically developed in the field of meat hygiene but should be viewed as a dynamic and challenging opportunity to review the packing house environment as it relates to the production of acceptable products, with a view to developing modified or new procedures that will facilitate the monitoring of a sanitation program.

Potential Contamination Sources

A control program is this area of sanitation requires a knowledge and understanding of the total environment in which meat products are handled. It further requires keen observation and constant review to assure that environmental influences have not arisen that could adversely affect the acceptability of the product. Look up, look down and look around, and examine the product itself.

Paint, Dust, Rust, Condensation and Disintegrating Insulating Material

The type of contamination can fall on or into product, equipment and packaging material. The sanitation program requires an ongoing campaign of good maintenance which will eliminate peeling paint, dust, rust, condensation and disintegrating insulating materials. Where overhead structures are so affected, it may be necessary to restrict the use of a room or an area. Equipment so affected must be withdrawn from use, until brought back into a satisfactory state.

Metal contaminants

Staples used for box forming operations are a real source of contamination. Box forming operations shall not be performed in close proximity to open containers of meat. Tag fasteners or skewers must be removed after serving their function and before carcasses are cut or boned. At no time are cleaning aids such as wire brushes or steel wool, to be used on meat products. It is further understood that they are not to be used in productions areas of a registered establishment, when meat products are present.

Metal contaminants may come from a multitude of other sources and may include the following: friction of metal hooks on overhead rails, beads and pieces of slag from welding equipment, poorly welded equipment, broken and worn equipment, can openers and containers, metal hangers, loose strapping, wires, etc.

The use of metal detectors should be encouraged in order to alert all concerned to the presence of metallic foreign material. The presence of metal in meat product is a serious situation which calls for a careful review of meat handling practices from slaughter through shipping of the product. Every effort must be expended to establish the source of the problem in order to rectify same.

Certain equipment and substances which generate gases or odours may have received approval for use from the Meat and Processed Animal Products Division. In many instances this approval has been conditional on a particular location, venting system or use. Other types of equipment such as mechanized vehicles do not require such approval. Inspectors must satisfy themselves that, in the case of the former group, the conditions are complied with and that in all instances the use of equipment and substances does not create a hazard to personnel, nor to meat products.

Other Types of Contaminants

These may include, but are not restricted to, the following: broken glass, packing paper, packing film, wood splinters, etc. Prevention consists of forbidding the use of glass, other than the product containers, in a processing area, the adequate defrosting of meat blocks in order to preclude the retention of wrapping paper and plastic films; assuring that the internal surfaces of meat transport vehicles are intact and free of wood splinters, that wooden skewers are not used as neck pins, etc. Any type of contamination requires a serious investigation on the part of management, in cooperation with inspection personnel, to establish the cause and to rectify same.

Where necessary, there must be adequate rinsing off of cleaning agents and disinfectants, and in addition, equipment surfaces subject to food contact must have all protective oil removed prior to use. Care must be taken that machinery and equipment lubricants do not contact or enter edible products in any manner. Much will depend on the placement of equipment such as motors.

Packaging Material

It is further required that the use of packaging materials be constantly reviewed from a functional standpoint. They must protect the product and not disintegrate, tear, etc. and thus, in themselves, become a contaminant. Cardboard containers must be stored and handled in a manner that minimizes contamination with dust, etc., and prevents contamination with liquids.

When packaging exposed meat products into unwaxed cardboard containers, liners must be used and every effort must be made to prevent the meat products from coming into contact with the exposed surfaces of the containers. When waxed cartons are used, contact with the external surfaces should be avoided. The packaging of exposed meat products into cardboard containers should not result in the external surfaces of the containers becoming stained with blood or fat.

Control of Wooden Pallets

Essentially, wooden pallets are permitted for use primarily in freezers and dry storages. The restriction results from the fact that wood is pervious to liquids and therefore difficult to clean. It is, however, realized that pallets must be loaded, unloaded and moved into areas, other than freezers and dry storages. This means that adequate control and judgement must be exercised to maintain the pallets free of contamination and damage which can adversely affect the level of sanitation in an establishment.

The onus rests with management to utilize pallets in a manner and in areas which prevent the creation of an unsanitary state; on this matter.Management must ensure that pallets are in good repair and clean before use. In some cases, where problems are encountered, the use will require restriction or change to appropriate alternate equipment.

Use of Products with Volatile Substrates

Certain paints, floor sealants, etc. contain a volatile element which may transfer an odour or chemical contamination to meat products. It is essential that areas treated with such products be adequately ventilated during and after the drying period, before meat products are permitted to enter those areas. It is recommended that the areas be closed off for a few hours, then a check for odours be made to ensure that complete dispersion has occurred.

Pre-operational Inspection

Hotel management is responsible for all aspects of quality control including the pre-operational inspection of all production areas. Management must assure that sanitary standards are met prior to permitting the commencement of operations.

The Meat Hygiene personnel monitors the effectiveness of management's sanitation program by periodically conducting inspections of the premises, facilities and equipment. The responsible inspector checks if control is being exercised over the environmental influences which may adversely affect meat or meat products processed therein.

The frequency of monitoring of the sanitaton program will be based on the known credibility of management to assume and perform their responsibilities. Room temperatures where refrigeration is a requirement must be at a correct level before the commencement of operations. A room temperature should, at this stage, be below the required level, since the movement of personnel into the room, plus their own body heat and the operation of sanitizers will cause the room temperature to rise.

Product contact zones are of immediate importance and would include table surfaces, equipment e.g. saws, and the interior of equipment. The latter shall be dismantled for ease of cleaning and not reassembled for use prior to receiving a pre-operational sanitary inspection.

Room surfaces such as floors, walls, ceilings and overhead fixtures are next in importance and must be maintained free of cracks and of rust, dust, and other extraneous material in addition to reasonable housekeeping practices. Condensation forming above product areas is not acceptable and this item must be covered on the pre-operational inspection.

The external and under-surfaces of equipment, such as product trucks, emulsifiers, mixers, etc., shall be examined for cleanliness. Such surfaces, if unclean, can serve as ready reservoirs for product contamination. The sanitation of employees' equipment, which may include knives, steels, hooks, mesh gloves, aprons, etc., is another responsibility of management. Sanitizers must be checked for the ability to function correctly at the required temperature.

It is to management's advantage to institute a check of effectiveness of their sanitation program by the use of bacteriological methods of review: e.g., Millipore, Swab Test or total plate count. Where deviations from accepted norms are found, management shall initiate the required action to remedy the situation. If the problem is not corrected, the use of equipment and/or facilities could be denied

OPERATIONAL INSPECTION

There is the added complication of the picture being confused by operations in progress. In addition, this facet of sanitation is a challenge, in that due to the rapidity of production, unacceptable practices could result in vast amounts of product out of compliance. Equipment, practices or services could be at fault.

The accumulation of proteinaceous material and fat on equipment over the course of a shift should be prevented as much as possible, but obviously this will occur within equipment in some locations where easy removal is not feasible. In order to reduce the hazard posed by such situations, adequate and correct temperature regulation is essential in order to slow down the reproduction rate of microorganisms.

Equipment such as sanitizers, hand washing facilities (including washrooms), etc. must be maintained in an acceptable fashion. Operating procedures, from the stunning of animals right through processing to shipping, must be performed with regard to alterations in the environment that would put the product at risk. Procedures must be constantly reviewed and examined for potential problems. On the kill floor, areas of common contact should be identified and sanitation procedures instituted. Prevention of contact with contaminated or diseased tissues is of prime importance.

Management must supply the required janitorial service (floor cleaning, trash removal, scrap removal, etc.) to maintain a satisfactory level of hygiene during operations. Also of importance are the work habits, dress and personal hygiene of employees. The inspector must be aware of and capable of detecting potential problems. He is further required to assure himself that management will initiate action to resolve the problems.

Sanitizers and Sanitizing Dips

Sanitizers, when strategically placed, maintained and utilized, become a very important facet of sanitation during daily operations. They must be sufficient in number and located where required. Management is required to assure that they are maintained and are functional prior to and during operations. Sanitizers must be operated at not less than 82C with adequate water overflow, in order to achieve a sufficient reduction in the number of microorganisms present.

It must be remembered that the presence of organic matter on the equipment will act as a barrier, thereby protecting the micro-organisms. Equipment should therefore be as clean as possible before it is placed in a sanitizer. When a chemical sanitizer is used in lieu of an 82°C water sanitizer, the sanitizing agent must be approved for this use and the manufacturers instructions on the label must be followed including contact time and rinsing or draining as applicable, and efficacy is demonstrated.

Hand sanitizing stations (e.g., dips, gels, sprays, etc.) serve as purposeful adjunct to the hand-washing facilities located in processing areas. They are required and must be used by all employees which come in direct contact with microbiologically sensitive meat products (ready-to-eat meat products). They must not be located where contamination of the product could occur.

They may be located next to the hand washing stations and used after hands have been thoroughly washed or closer to the production line where no contamination of product or direct contact surfaces can occur. The use of hand sanitizing solutions must be restricted to those listed in the Reference Listing of Accepted Construction Materials, Packaging Materials and Non-Food Chemical Products.

It is further required that they be used in keeping with directions on the label (eg: correct concentration, contact time). The hand dip solutions should be renewed throughout the day, as often as necessary, so that they, in themselves, do not become a source of contamination. Caution must be exercised in that management and inspection personnel do not put excessive reliance on this aspect of sanitation, to the detriment of other sanitary control measures throughout the operations.

Relaxation of sanitary requirements earlier in the production process cannot be offset by the ritualistic dunking of hands. Antibacterial soaps can be used in place of hand sanitizing dips. These soaps must be listed in the Reference Listing of Accepted Construction Materials, Packaging Materials and Non-Food Chemical Products and be used according to the directions on the label. Plastic gloves may be worn by employees which come in direct contact with ready-to-eat meat products as long as their hands are washed upon entering the processing area, prior to putting the gloves on, and their gloved hands are sanitized in an approved hand dip prior to handling product.

Exemptions to Refrigeration Requirements

The following rules supersede and replace all previously existing exemptions to refrigeration requirements for processing rooms. Note that temperature requirements for storage rooms, curing rooms and non-production areas are not changed. Therefore, these rules do not apply to:

— Cooking rooms (e.g., oven, kettles, fryers, etc.);

— Fermentation and aging rooms;

— Transfer areas into and out of cook rooms (e.g. hallways where no product is kept);

— kill floors, evisceration floors, scalding rooms and slaughter associated processes such as tripe, feet, casings, etc.

As a general rule, all meat product processing operations (including those for shelf stable dry cured meat products having "keep refrigerated" on the label) shall be conducted in refrigerated rooms (i.e., maintained at a temperature of 10°C or less).

Exemptions from the requirement to maintain refrigeration (10°C) in processing rooms can be granted by a Regional Program Manager, Meat Hygiene, if ALL of the following conditions (A,B,C and D) are met:

A. The environment (equipment, contact surfaces, handlers.) shall not pose a risk of product contamination at any time during operations. Each HACCP- based QC program shall be reviewed and recommended by a team composed of the Inspector-in-Charge and a regional program specialist having the required specialized knowledge, then submitted to a Regional Program Manager, Meat Hygiene.

   After appropriate review by the Regional Program Manager, the program will be stamped and returned to the operator with the reviewers' conclusions. The operator must keep any letter of acceptance on file for future reference and review by the Inspector-in-Charge. As each process will be inherently different, it is impossible to provide set microbiological guidelines suitable for all operations. Microbiological programs will therefore need to be developed by the operator on a case by case basis to the satisfaction of the Regional Program Manager, Meat Hygiene and shall demonstrate the safety of the environment at all times during processing.

B. Any unclean equipment that was previously used and left unused for a period of 2 hours or more shall be completely taken apart, cleansed and sanitized before being reused;

C. Unless the operator is able to demonstrate the continual microbiological acceptability of the environment (by means of a valid microbiological sampling program), a complete mid-shift clean up (including equipment dismantling) of contact surfaces shall take place at least once every 4 hours during operations.

   Such a mid-shift cleanup procedure shall consist of removal of all meat products, other ingredients and packaging material from the room prior to conducting a thorough cleaning and sanitation of product contact surfaces. Should such cleaning create condensation on overhead structures, the condensate must be eliminated prior to the start-up of operations. At the end of a mid-shift clean-up, product contact surfaces shall meet the same criteria as for the pre-operational inspection stage.

Formulation operations

An exception for the refrigeration of formulation rooms under specific circumstances has been made. Most meat products entering these rooms come directly from the cooler and are at a relatively low temperature. All formulation, stuffing, handling, pre-blending, marination, etc. operations involved in the processing of meat products are eligible for exemption from refrigeration requirements provided all of the following additional conditions are met:

— the meat used in the product was either hot boned immediately prior to processing OR previously chilled to a temperature of 4°C. or less, and

— the meat surface temperature never exceeds 7°C; and

— in the case of a non-cured product, cooking (product must be fully cooked), drying or fermenting of the product shall start within 2 hours of the time it first enters a non refrigerated area.

— In the case of a cured product, cooking (product must be fully cooked), drying or fermenting of the product shall start within 4 hours of the time it first enters a non refrigerated area.

Comminuting operations

Comminuting operations (e.g., grinding, emulsifying, dicing, slicing, chopping, etc. of raw meat products) are eligible for exemption from refrigeration requirements provided all of the following additional conditions are met:

— The meat to be comminuted was previously chilled to 4°C or less and

— the comminuted product cooking cycle is initiated within 2 hours from the time the product enters a non refrigerated area.

Meat filled pastries

The processing of meat-filled pastries and meat-filled pasta (e.g., ravioli, tortellini, etc.) that cannot technically be processed under refrigeration (because the dough will not stick together in a refrigerated area), as well as continuous lines for breaded meat products, could be allowed in a nonrefrigerated area provided all of the following conditions are met:

— the meat product has been chilled to a temperature of 4°C. or less before being transferred to the nonrefrigerated area AND the meat product surface temperature does not exceed 7°C. at any time during the process; and

— the product is either:

  — placed in a freezer within 30 minutes after the preparation is completed or

  — fully cooked or pasteurized within 30 minutes after the preparation is completed and subsequently chilled or frozen.

Assembling and packaging of meat products

Different situations could occur with different levels of risk:

Packaging of cooked refrigerated (4°C or less) meat products shall be done in a refrigerated room (maximum temperature of 10°C) in order to minimize reheating of product surfaces and possible growth of pathogens.

Packaging of frozen meat products in a non refrigerated room could be allowed if:

— The product enters the nonrefrigerated room in a frozen condition; and

— the product's surface temperature does not exceed 0°C. while in the nonrefrigerated packaging room.

Assembly and packaging of entrées, such as pizzas and TV dinners could be allowed in a nonrefrigerated room provided all of the following conditions are met:

— The process is continuous in nature;

— The meat product has been chilled to a temperature of 4°C. or less before being transferred to the nonrefrigerated area; and the product's surface temperature does not exceed a temperature of 7°C. at any time during the process;

Handling and packaging of dry soup mixes, bouillons, broths, concentrates, tallow, lard, suet, edible casing preparation, edible fat and shelf stable dry cured meats:

Because these products are shelf stable and represent a very low health risk, an exemption could be granted. Please note that the handling (e.g., boning, picking, dicing, etc.) of warm cooked meat product when those products could be used as ready-to-eat products (e.g. diced chicken that could be used for salads) is not exempted and shall therefore be conducted in a fully refrigerated area.

It should be remembered that unless the operator is able to demonstrate the continual microbiological acceptability of the environment, a thorough and complete mid-shift clean up and a preoperational check shall take place at least once every 4 hours of operations. Some discretion is permitted when dealing with enclosed equipment through which product is passing on an almost continuous basis, e.g. stuffers. In these instances, dismantling and cleaning may be permitted on a daily rather than a shift basis.

Mid-shift clean-up

The only other case where a mid-shift clean-up procedure is allowed in lieu of adequate refrigeration is when there has been a temporary mechanical failure of refrigeration equipment making it impossible to maintain the prescribed room temperature. In this case, measures must be taken to ensure that product temperatures do not exceed 10°C.

This may be accomplished by icing, or other satisfactory means. In those cases where the prescribed room temperature cannot be maintained, a thorough cleanup must be made after each four hours of operation.

Such a mid-shift clean-up procedure must consist of removal of all meat products, other ingredients and packaging materials from the room prior to a thorough cleaning of product contact surfaces and a rinse down of floor areas. Should such cleaning create condensation on overhead structures, the condensate must be eliminated prior to the start-up of operations.

Outside Premises

This is an area which often does not receive the attention it deserves. The location of a hotel in conjunction with the sanitation of the external premises has a bearing on sanitation with the premises. The standard of sanitation practised outside the premises may well be reflected in the attitude of hotel employees within the establishment.

Consistent implementation of good groundkeeping habits is required to prevent product contamination from objectionable odours, vermin, ash, dust, etc.. Programs must be developed for the storage and removal of unwanted material. Suitable storage facilities must be provided for garbage which should be removed daily. Meat and bone scraps require proper containers and refrigeration to prevent a potential hazard from flies and bacteria.

Unused and obsolete equipment, building materials, etc. must not be allowed to accumulate in disarray but should be piled neatly and routinely removed if of no further use. Grass and weeds should be kept under control. The location of an incinerator, if permitted by local authorities, should be such that the prevailing winds do not direct the fumes or smoke toward the hotel. The incinerator must be placed on a suitable concrete foundation and fitted with a screen to control the emission of flying ash.

Transportation of Finished Products

The vehicle used in the transport of meat products is technically an extension of the hotel premises. When examined or considered in this light it is obvious that the vehicle acts as the interim storage facility from the hotel to its point of destination. Acceptance of this premise dictates that construction, maintenance, sanitation and refrigeration standards must equate, as closely as is reasonably possible, to those standards required of the registered establishment.

Management is required to assume the responsibility of providing satisfactory conveyance vehicles and mechanisms for the transport of meat product. Inspection personnel are required to monitor this aspect of hotel operations and are further empowered to deny the use of unsatisfactory vehicles and to hold for reworking or refuse entry to products received in unsatisfactory vehicles or which have been subjected to abuse, e.g., defrosting, contamination, etc. during transportation.

Animal Transportation and Holding Pens

The vehicles and crates used to transport animals to slaughter play an important role, not only in the humane treatment of animals and the control of animal disease, but also in sanitation. In general, the cleaner animals are upon reaching the slaughter floor, the better the chances of reducing contamination levels on dressed carcasses, assuming good dressing practices are put to use.

To encourage those transporting animals to load them into clean vehicles and crates, it is important that a good example be set, by ensuring that all vehicles and crates leaving a registered establishment are cleaned and disinfected in accordance with the Health of Animals Act and Regulations.

Construction and design should be such that this area may be kept reasonably free of manure, straw, odour, etc., that may attract and harbour insect and rodent populations. Total sanitation is further enhanced through the provision of adequately lighted "held pens" for reactor and suspect animals in order to isolate them from other animals.

A cleaning and disinfecting program should be developed in keeping with the operations and disease control requirements, e.g., reator pens to be cleaned and disinfected after each day's use or more frequently, if directed. Routine cleaning shall be performed as often as is necessary to meet the objectives as outlined above.

Good animal husbandry must be manifested in the provision of clean feed, water and bedding, where necessary. Implicit in good husbandry practices is the maintenance of the facility so that it is free of exposed nails, broken boards, floors, etc. that may injure the animals.

Waste Disposal

It is preferable that waste such as paper, boxes, strings, etc. be removed from the hotel premises on a daily basis. Properly identified containers designed for holding this material must be provided throughout the hotel. Janitorial service is to be supplied, that will remove and replace these containers as often as necessary. Overflow and spillage on the floor defeats their purpose. Attention to detail in this area of hotel sanitation helps create an atmosphere and attitude that is reflected in employees' work attitudes. A sloppy work place begets sloppy work habits.

Waste materials within the livestock pens, such as manure and straw, may be collected and deposited on a hard surfaced slab for subsequent removal. A program must be initiated for the routine removal of this material so as to prevent the possibility of its becoming a harbouring place for flies and vermin and giving rise to objectionable odours.

*Disposal of condemned and other inedible meat products*Control of this aspect of packing house sanitation is of vital importance. Every effort must be made to assure that the storage and handling of these materials does not put edible products at risk.

Segregation is the key to control: This is achieved through developing an acceptable flow system, so that inedible meat product is directed away from the edible meat product. Part of this system may be appropriately marked containers or chutes used to move product to the designated inedible and condemned product rooms of an establishment.

The identity of these products must be maintained at all times until they are used as animal food products or, in the case of condemned material, until they are subjected to a sterilization process or disposed of in accordance with the Meat Inspection Regulations. These products should always move directly to their designated areas and should never be rerouted through the processing areas used for edible products. Odour in the hotel from inedible operations may indicate an error in the pattern of air flow.

The equipment used for the handling of these products must be frequently cleaned and disinfected and any equipment returning into edible areas must first be cleaned. The storage areas or rooms must also be subject to a scrupulous cleaning and sanitizing program. This equipment and the storage facilities represent a very real sanitation hazard to the establishment, if not subjected to a rigid sanitation control program.

Welfare Facilities

The provision of adequate welfare facilities is an indispensable requirement for the promotion of hygienic practices. The quality of facilities provided to employees in this area of their work environment is so often reflected in their attitude and work habits relating to sanitation at the work stations. Attention must be paid to the size, lighting, ventilation, etc.

These facilities must be maintained and provided with adequate janitorial service throughout the day. Close attention must be paid to the possible infestation with vermin, e.g., cockroaches. Failure to respond to the needs and standards in these areas may require withdrawal of inspection privileges until rectification of the deficiencies has been accomplished.

Personal Hygiene of Hotel Employees and Inspection Staff

Hotel management is responsible for an ongoing educational program that will inform all employees of their responsibilities in this aspect of sanitation. Management has a further responsibility of assuring that the requirements are being consistently met by their employees in the interest of the quality of the product and the well-being of their staff. The following is important in all areas where edible products or ingredients are handled, prepared or stored and where equipment and utensils are washed.

Sanitary Work Habits

These shall preclude the use of chewing gum, snuff and tobacco in any form in production areas. Eating and drinking shall be confined to the designated lunch room areas, except that water from fountains may be consumed in production areas.

Hands, including fingernails, shall be clean and shall be washed at all times after using the lavatory facilities. Hand wash facilities are to be located at the entrances to production areas are used by everyone upon entering the food production/handling area. By making these visible, thus enabling their use to be monitored, additional safeguards with respect to hand washing are provided. Scratching of the head, face, etc., or the placing of fingers in or around the mouth or nose are not acceptable practices.

Care of the hands shall include the treatment and appropriate covering of all cuts and sores by the hotel nurse or designated first aid employee. The use of hand creams and lotions shall be restricted to and in keeping with the label instructions of those "Accepted for Use" by the Meat and Processed Animal Products Division. One must avoid the use of nail polish when handling edible product.

Working Apparel

Common sense will have to be used by hotel employees and inspection staff when interpreting these guidelines; what is important to remember is that the intent of the policy is to protect the meat product from all possible sources of contamination.

The Department's policy regarding work clothing is to prevent contamination of edible products by contact with clothing of questionable cleanliness. In order to prevent this form of contamination, suitably washed and maintained work clothing must be substituted for or worn over any other piece of clothing that may contact food products. Work clothing must not be worn or stored in incompatible areas (washrooms, lunchrooms, lockers used for street clothing, outside the hotel, etc.).

Employees that must enter areas of the hotel which are incompatible (eg: barn/slaughter floor, maintenance staff) take appropriate measures to prevent cross-contamination (eg: coded smocks, cover garments). Employees in ready-to-eat product areas remove their outer garments before leaving the area and hang them in designated areas.

Overalls are not considered to be acceptable work clothing for employees handling edible exposed meat products. Footwear should be of a design and material that is equal to the challenge of the work environment. The eviscerator's boots, where he is working on a moving top table, shall be of a material impervious to moisture and shall be of a colour distinct from other footwear. These boots must be worn only at the work station. Other footwear must be utilized when walking to and from the work station. These boots, along with aprons, knives and associated gear, must be cleaned and sanitized in the adjacent boot cleaning compartment.

Personal adornment and accessories to clothing such as jewelry, badges, buttons, create a potential risk to meat products and, at times, create a risk to the safety of the employee where moving equipment is involved. All such items shall not be worn in food preparation and packaging areas. In these same areas, items such as pens, pencils, thermometers, etc., should not be kept in coat/shirt pockets where they may accidently fall into products.

Jewellery items which cannot be removed such as continuous loop earrings, weddings bands, medic alert bracelets or necklaces, etc., also create a potential risk to the safety of the product and must be adequately covered. Facial adornments that cannot be removed or are not removed because of any reason (e.g. religious, cultural, etc.), are items which have the potential to fall or otherwise contaminate the meat product if they are improperly attached.

In view of the fact that these adornments pose a food safety hazard and that it is impracticable to verify if they are worn securely, they shall be either removed or adequately covered when worn in food preparation and packaging areas. The proper use of hairnets or other appropriate headcover and gloves to cover personal adornments, or surgical masks in the case of facial adornments, would be considered adequate cover. A "bandaid", however, used to cover a wedding band is inadequate, as it cannot be cleaned and may become dislodged and further contribute to product contamination.

Protective gear such as helmets, wrist guards, aprons, steel-meshed gloves, etc. must be of materials capable of being cleaned and maintained clean. All such equipment must be cleaned and sanitized immediately if they meet with gross contamination during operations (e.g., ruptured abscess during postmortem operations). The use of cloth gloves is to be discouraged due to the fact that they rapidly become soiled and, subsequently, can easily contaminate meat products. Should cloth gloves be worn on the slaughter floor, tripe wash area or other similar operation, they must be covered by an accepted impervious material. The use of uncovered cloth gloves may be permitted only in boning and cutting or similar operations, where safety may be a factor.

However, such use should be minimized and, preferably, the gloves should be covered by an accepted impervious material. However, if the policy of the operator is to change cloth gloves at every two hours of operation or less, and such a policy is effectively controlled by the operator, such use will be permitted. In cases where the use of cloth gloves cannot be effectively controlled by the operator and meat products are being contaminated, the use of such gloves will have to be denied or they will have to be covered by an accepted impervious material. The use of cloth gloves to handle exposed, ready-to-eat meat products is not permitted.

All persons working or entering areas where food products are open to exposure must wear appropriate head coverings, to prevent the contamination of the product through the introduction of falling hair. In order to achieve this, the head coverings must cover all exposed hair. If hairnets are used, the mesh must be small enough to adequately stop loose hair from escaping. Hairnets must also be used to cover all exposed facial hair with the sole exception of neatly trimmed moustaches. Head coverings must be maintained clean and be in a good state of repair.

Work clothing and equipment such as knives, hooks, steels, mesh gloves, etc. is preferably stored in a central location, at or near the work stations. At the end of operations, all such equipment should be cleaned and sanitized and be available for a pre-operational inspection. This control is weakened when such equipment is stored in each employee's locker. If security for personal working tools is required, separate lockers are preferable. If this equipment is stored away from the work site a formal inspection procedure must be instituted to examine the equipment as it is brought into the production area.

Vermin Control

Satisfactory hotel construction in keeping with an excellent housekeeping program, along with the use of screens, air curtains, and electrical insect control devices are the first steps in avoiding the introduction of insects and rodents.

Vermin, through their habits, are capable of introducing serious human diseases to food products. Their use is indicated where other measures have failed to keep out vermin. Their use must not be a substitute for satisfactory hotel construction or housekeeping.

Responsibility for Use

This rests with hotel management. To this end, it is required that only licensed pest control operators or designated hotel employees, under adequate inspection control, may prepare and use such materials.

Insecticides

These may be residual or non-residual. They may take the form of aerosols, sprays, powders, pellets, repellents or gases. Each may be specifically formulated for designated use and places. The inspection staff should be aware of the insecticides being used and of any potential restrictions for their use or application.

Rodenticides

These may come in dry form or liquid form and be presented in a variety of bait stations. It is imperative that these stations be identified and that a map of their location be in the possession of the inspection staff. It is important that these stations be adequately serviced and supervised. All stations must be of the covered variety. All bait stations must be removed from edible product rooms and areas before the commencement of operations.

The inspection staff should be aware of the rodenticides being used and the lo-cation of bait stations throughout the hotel. Management or their agents must provide the inspector in charge with a map locating every bait station, and provide a regular report on the control program to the inspector in charge.

STORAGE OF HAZARDOUS NON-FOOD CHEMICALS

There are occasions when hazardous non-food chemicals such as rodenticides, herbicides, etc. are stored in registered establishments. Such situations have the potential to lead to accidental misuse or contamination of meat products. Although correct labelling of all non food items is required, complete reliance cannot be placed on this as a control measure, owing to the varying degrees of literacy encountered amongst company employees.

— Where feasible, hazardous non food chemicals are to be stored away from registered establishments and only required amounts be brought onto the premises under the direct supervision of a responsible company employee.

— Such materials, if it is necessary to store them on the premises, are to be stored in a separate room or partitioned area of a storage room, under lock and key, with controlled access being given to a responsible individual or small group of company employees.

— If either of the above is not possible, then such materials are to be stored, well separated from other non food items, in such a manner that accidental misuse or contamination is prevented.

— Where hazardous chemicals are stored in a registered establishment, the use of a colour coding or similar type of system is strongly recommended to enable company personnel to identify different categories of product.

Since the amount of space available, alternative sites for storage, etc. will vary considerably between different establishment, it is the responsibility of inspection staff and hotel managements to jointly review individual situations and where necessary, take action to ensure good control and security. All of the above measures are additional to, and not a substitute for, existing measures such as divisional acceptance, labelling and monitoring of use by inspection staff.

NON-MEAT INGREDIENTS

Management must have written specifications for all non-meat ingredients to prevent biological, chemical and physical hazards in food. Storage of such products shall be maintained in designated dry storage areas or spice rooms in the establishment. Such areas or rooms shall be free of excessive moisture. Products of this nature are to be considered as edible products and shall be supported on racks or pallets in keeping with acceptable practices.

A high standard of housekeeping is required in these areas. It is further understood that non-food chemicals such as soaps, detergents, etc. shall not be stored in these areas. In addition every effort must be undertaken to store and secure these non-meat ingredients free from dust, rodents and insects. To this end it is recommended that properly designed and lidded containers be utilized where practical.

Unwashed vegetables must be stored, washed and prepared in separate rooms and areas to prevent the introduction of contamination. The inspector's responsibility in non-meat product handling areas is to ensure that a satisfactory environmental sanitation level is maintained, which will not jeopardize meat products. Actual production procedures, regulatory standards and labelling lie of our jurisdiction.

When opening containers such as bags, sacks, etc., care should be exercised so that this is performed away from the meat products to which their contents are to be added, in order to preclude the inadvertent admission of extraneous material such as string, sacking material, fibres of paper, dust, etc. This is in essence, the development of work habits and practices that lend themselves to the prevention of the introduction of extraneous material to the meat food products.

ACCEPTABLE MATERIALS AND AGENTS

Management and inspection personnel are to be guided by the Meat and Poultry Products Division Reference Listing of Acceptable Materials and Agents. It is hotel managment's responsibility to demonstrate that all such materials and agents are being used in keeping with instructions on the label and thereby avoiding misuse of a product which could possibly put an edible food product at risk.

Management and inspection personnel should further satisfy themselves that the pro-duct, when used, is effective for its intended purpose and that its use does not create some unforeseen problem. Equipment and hotel layout map change, as may hotel processing procedures, and hotel personnel. Constant vigilance is in order, as many materials and agents contain toxic ingredients that could create a very serious risk for the hotel environment and the meat products produced there in. The judicious use of such products cannot be too strongly emphasized. Control mechanism must be instituted as follows:

— Management must keep the inspection staff advised as to the chemical compounds in use at the establishment; and

— Veterinarians or inspectors in charge must have in their possession an up-to-date list of all chemicals being utilized in the operation, such as hand soaps, cleaner, lubricants, pesticides, etc., with particular reference to those used in production areas or those likely to cause product contamination.

Bibliography

Babcock, Emma Whitcomb. *Household hints*. New York: D. Appleton and company, 1881.

Balderston, Lydia Ray. *Housekeeping handbook*, how to do it. Chicago, Philadelphia etc.: J. B. Lippincott company, 1944.

____________. *Housekeeping workbook how to do it--house care and cleaning*. Chicago, Philadelphia: J. B. Lippincott company, 1935.

Baxter, Lucia Allen Millet. *Housekeepers handy book*. Boston and New York: Houghton Mifflin company, 1913.

Butterworth, Annie. *Manual of household work and management*. London New York etc.: Longmans Green and Co., 1935.

Campbell, Helen. *The housekeeper's year-book*. New York: Fords Howard & Hulbert, 1882.

Colson, Elizabeth, Anna Gansevoort Chittenden, and Alice R. Baldwin. *The child housekeeper; simple lessons, with songs, stories, and games*. New York: A. S. Barnes and company, 1903.

Cooley, Anna Maria and Wilhelmina H. Spohr. *Household arts for home and school*. New York: Macmillan, 1920.

Dewing, M. O. *From attic to cellar: a book for young housekeepers*. New York: Putnam, 1879.

Diaz, Abby Morton. *Domestic problems: work and culture in the household, and the schoolmaster's trunk*. Boston: James R. Osgood, 1881.

Ellet, E. F. *The new cyclopedia of domestic economy, and practical housekeeper; adapted to all classes of society, and comprising subjects connected with the interests of every family*. Norwich Ct.: Henry Bill, 1872.

Fales, Winnifred Shaw. *The easy housekeeping book*. Boston: Small Maynard & company, 1923.

Fleming, Mary Elizabeth Lee. *Emergency helps for housekeepers and others*. Lynchburg Va.: J. P. Bell printers, 1906.

Gilman, Caroline Howard. *Recollections of a housekeeper*. New-York: Harper & Brothers, 1834.

Haweis, Mary Eliza. *The art of housekeeping: a bridal garland*. London: Sampson Low Marston Searle & Rivington, 1889.

Jones, Gladys Beckett. *Manual of smart housekeeping*. New York: C. R. Heck, 1946.

Index